SpringerBriefs in Education

We are delighted to announce SpringerBriefs in Education, an innovative product type that combines elements of both journals and books. Briefs present concise summaries of cutting-edge research and practical applications in education. Featuring compact volumes of 50 to 125 pages, the SpringerBriefs in Education allow authors to present their ideas and readers to absorb them with a minimal time investment. Briefs are published as part of Springer's eBook Collection. In addition, Briefs are available for individual print and electronic purchase.

SpringerBriefs in Education cover a broad range of educational fields such as: Science Education, Higher Education, Educational Psychology, Assessment & Evaluation, Language Education, Mathematics Education, Educational Technology, Medical Education and Educational Policy.

SpringerBriefs typically offer an outlet for:

- An introduction to a (sub)field in education summarizing and giving an overview of theories, issues, core concepts and/or key literature in a particular field
- A timely report of state-of-the art analytical techniques and instruments in the field of educational research
- A presentation of core educational concepts
- An overview of a testing and evaluation method
- A snapshot of a hot or emerging topic or policy change
- An in-depth case study
- A literature review
- A report/review study of a survey
- An elaborated thesis

Both solicited and unsolicited manuscripts are considered for publication in the SpringerBriefs in Education series. Potential authors are warmly invited to complete and submit the Briefs Author Proposal form. All projects will be submitted to editorial review by editorial advisors.

SpringerBriefs are characterized by expedited production schedules with the aim for publication 8 to 12 weeks after acceptance and fast, global electronic dissemination through our online platform SpringerLink. The standard concise author contracts guarantee that:

- an individual ISBN is assigned to each manuscript
- each manuscript is copyrighted in the name of the author
- the author retains the right to post the pre-publication version on his/her website or that of his/her institution

Juliet Aleta Rivera Villanueva ·
Douglas Charles Forbes Eacersall

Autoethnographic Reflections on a Research Journey

Dual Perspectives from a Doctoral Student and a Researcher Development Specialist

 Springer

Juliet Aleta Rivera Villanueva ⓘ
Faculty of Education
University of the Philippines Open
University
Laguna, Philippines

Douglas Charles Forbes Eacersall ⓘ
University of the Philippines Open
University
Laguna, Philippines

University of Southern Queensland
Toowoomba, Australia

ISSN 2211-1921 ISSN 2211-193X (electronic)
SpringerBriefs in Education
ISBN 978-981-99-4928-1 ISBN 978-981-99-4929-8 (eBook)
https://doi.org/10.1007/978-981-99-4929-8

This Springer imprint is published by the registered company Springer Nature Singapore Pte Ltd.
The registered company address is: 152 Beach Road, #21-01/04 Gateway East, Singapore 189721, Singapore

Dedicated to our parents,
Julieta and Manuel
Patricia and Jeffrey

Acknowledgments

We would like to thank our universities for giving us the time and space to undertake this project. We are also thankful to our colleagues, the research support team, reviewers, research advisers, and friends for their presence in our lives as academics.

Of worthy mention are the members of the Research and Writing League who are just as supportive and excited with our project coming into fruition during the pandemic. Our special thanks also go to Grace Ma and Rajan Muthu for their guidance throughout the early and final stages of this publication.

Our heartfelt appreciation to friends and family, the superheroes of our lives, for their love, care, and humanity.

Contents

List of Figures

Introduction

Abstract This introductory chapter outlines our approach to investigating research student experience and associated identity issues using a collaborative autoethnographic approach. The theories used to understand and analyze the research student journey—the Community of Inquiry framework, identity theory, and identity-trajectory theory are also explained, and the main themes, including the research journey as an expression of the self; a reflective practice; a rite of passage; and as a collaborative act, are identified. These themes demonstrate the importance of the self and others in the conceptualization of the research topic, approaches to research student development and training, supervision, learning thresholds and states of liminality, learning alliances and collaborative research cultures, and the supports that help to ensure research student success, identity development, and wellbeing.

Keywords Doctoral education · Research student · Student experience · Student success · Researcher identity · HDR · Higher degree by research · Postgraduate research · PGR

This book has been a joy to write. Personal reflections on a research journey, shared with a friend and colleague, bring back fond memories of the high times as well as the times of struggle. The story discusses the following themes: the research journey as an expression of the self; a reflective practice; a rite of passage; and a collaborative act. The first three of these themes cover the early aspects of the journey when the main storyteller, a PhD student, traveled alone. The last two were experienced with a traveling companion, who is a researcher development specialist and the co-author. This book uses autoethnography to reflect and deepen analysis of the doctoral research journey through the lens of identity and, specifically, identity-trajectory from both the personal and academic lifespan covering a range of doctoral research experiences. To formally start this autoethnographic account we would like to introduce ourselves, the two main characters: Aleta and Douglas.

Aleta: Before attending one of Douglas' research training sessions on writing abstracts, I searched my email for specific abstracts and paper submissions since 2008. I found a paper close to my heart because the writing was quite therapeutic. It was my first autoethnography on coming to terms with the pressures of a new job title, 'Assistant Professor and Program Chair', at a university in my home country—the Philippines. I wasn't sure whether my writing was autoethnographic enough, so I kept it as a writing experiment. Who would be interested in issues and concerns of a novice faculty member, and a middle-aged early career researcher at that? Imagine having to reveal on-the-job moments of uncertainty and self-doubt in the top university of my home country. No way. And yet, in 2019 during my third year, with 'PhD Candidate, Assistant Professor (on study leave)' indicated under my name, a voice, itchy to my brain, was nudging me to return to autoethnography, but this time in relation to my doctoral research journeys—version 1 (PhD v.1.0) and version 2 (PhD v.2.0). I thought three years of being in a happy space, undertaking my PhD v.2.0 as an international student in Australia, should be a good time to write an autoethnographic narrative. During this sojourn, I regained my confidence to dare test these waters of uncertainty again, knowing instinctively that I would survive, have fun in the process, and if not, laugh at my self-doubts and tunnel-vision moments. After all, I have survived a track record of four university application rejections, a low pass for my PhD v.1.0 comprehensive exams, two near death experiences at sea, and one truly embarrassing moment in this earthly life. Writing on my journey should be one step toward my dream of being in a remote beach camp, with my constant other, wearing only our wedding rings ten years from now. In other words, from this day till then, I really have nothing to lose having lost myself quite a few times already. I will stay afloat and enjoy the swim.

Through this autoethnographic study, I'd like to look back and reflect on the constraints, motivations, and enablers which led me to the dissertation phase of my journey, successful completion, and a return to my academic work responsibilities. My initial ideas for this autoethnography were triggered during a Postgraduate and Early Career Research (PGECR) meeting at the Australian university where I was undertaking my PhD v.2.0. The presenter relayed varied responses regarding why people pursued their doctoral study. In response, I blogged about my own reasons for pursuing my research project. While I concluded by saying my journey can be categorized under the presenter's theme 'to prove a point', I had not quite explored what that really meant. The PGECR symposium convened by Douglas, as seen below, seemed to me a safe space to share my story given ideas identified as "research as a bittersweet journey; barriers and enablers" under the symposium theme which resonated well with my experiences (Fig. 1).

As seen in the below digital artifact, received by email, for the PGECR symposium, there was a clear call for engagement on the themes which to me relate well with the doctoral student journey. Also, the idea of being able to connect with 'all fields of research' was quite new to me. Hence, I decided to engage Douglas' assistance and advice through an autoethnography sounding board email thread to embark on the actual (re)writing and (re)telling of my story while immersed in the critical stage of writing my doctoral dissertation. Under the email subject: "auto-ethKNOW sounding board", we corresponded by email over a few months to help me understand ways I could shape the autoethnographic writing of my foreseen presentation.

Invitation

You are warmly invited to participate in the
**24th Postgraduate and Early Career Researcher
(PGECR) Group research symposium.**

Date: Friday, 15 November 2019
Time: 9am-5pm (followed by symposium dinner)
Location: QLD Campus (and via Zoom – link to be provided after registration)

The symposium theme is
Paradoxes of research: The contradictions, conundrums and celebrations.

Research paradoxes exist across all disciplines and methodologies. The following examples are not exhaustive, but are provided to provoke presentation ideas: planning vs flexibility; sampling vs generalising, researcher as expert vs novice; comprehensive summary; privilege and social justice; conventions vs pushing boundaries; research as a bittersweet journey; barriers and enablers; eliminating bias. Authors of abstracts are invited to engage with any elements of the theme and sub-themes.

If you have any questions or if you would like to present a paper, please send a title and abstract (150-200 words) to **Douglas Eacersall**
by **5pm Friday, 20 September 2019.**

**Please ensure that your presentation abstract
aligns with the symposium theme.**

Symposium presentations can take a variety of formats, including but not limited to:

• Conceptual papers • Debates • Empirical papers • Sharing research data
• Methodological papers • Performances• Provocations

Presentations may engage with the symposium theme in a number of ways and you are welcome to present research that is at any stage or development, from conception through to reflection. After all, as researchers we are always undertaking particular journeys in the pursuit of new knowledge, creativity and thought. All fields of research are welcome, as are all levels of research experience.

Fig. 1 Screenshot of the PGECR Symposium eFlyer. *Note.* Adapted from Villanueva (personal communication, September 2019)

Douglas: I am an academic and researcher development specialist at a small regional university in Australia. In this role, I have the privilege of assisting research students with their research studies. I first met Aleta at a research writing bootcamp I was facilitating and from that moment participated in various stages of her doctoral studies during her research journey PhD v.2.0. My role in Aleta's studies was one of providing advice and support at particular moments in her research journey. My role in this book is similar. Just as the PhD was Aleta's, so is this story. It is her journey but a journey I had the pleasure to share in. Throughout this work, I collaborated with Aleta to curate and 'unpack' the autoethnographic artifacts. I have also provided commentary and elaboration at key moments, drawing on my own doctoral studies and experiences as a lecturer in research training and development.

My own PhD was undertaken from 2012 to 2018 in the field of sports history, examining the revival and reconstruction of western martial pursuits in Australia from 1969 to 2016. This was an unusual but interesting topic and one certainly worth the effort to uncover. My experience of doctoral study was a happy but difficult one. Undertaking a research degree can be a bumpy road with potholes, forests, mountains, and sometimes no road at all to navigate the way. I appreciate the efforts of researchers, especially student researchers, who strive earnestly to make an original and significant contribution to knowledge. It is not always an easy journey, but it is usually a worthwhile one.

In my role, I assist student researchers to use tools and effective strategies that make the research journey easier and more fulfilling. I have been in this position since 2015, and over this time I have had numerous interactions with research students across all disciplines. I have provided advice on supervisory team management, project conceptualization, project management, critical thinking, literature reviews, information management, critical reading, time management, note taking, academic writing, structuring the thesis, and personal issues. I feel privileged to have shared in the tears of frustration, as well as the triumphs of passing important milestones, as I have traveled the road with each student. It is a role that sometimes makes me feel like Batman—a mere mortal employing the tools of research to help students as they travel around and through research city. It is my hope that this book will assist research students through all parts of their journey and most importantly that it will enable them to reflect on their own journey and the realization that they are not alone.

What We Hope to Achieve

There are many factors involved in the student research journey, each of which can affect student experience. These factors include financial pressures (Beasy et al., 2021; Sverdlik et al., 2018), administrative processes (Beasy et al., 2021), ethical research approval processes (Carniel et al., 2022; Hickey et al., 2022), effective research supervision (Scott & Takarangi, 2019, Sverdlik et al., 2018), the global COVID-19 pandemic (Brownlow et al., 2022), successfully identifying student needs (Eacersall, 2018), writing competency (Sverdlik et al., 2018), issues with researcher and academic identity (Carter et al., 2013; Coffman et al., 2016; Koole & Stack, 2016; Pifer & Baker, 2016; Sverdlik et al., 2018), and developing a viable project to meet requirements like Confirmation of Candidature (Bartlett & Eacersall, 2019). These issues can have significant impacts on student success, student experience and individual student wellbeing (Beasy et al., 2021; Guthrie et al., 2017; Sverdlik et al., 2018). Although there is a growing area of research regarding these issues and their impact on student experience, more research is needed, especially in terms of how students might be supported (Pretorius, 2019) in order to foster positive student experiences and the development of well-rounded researcher identities. More focus is also needed on the under-researched area of first-year research student experience especially in terms of research project feasibility and topic conceptualization (for dated examples see Hockey, 1994; Wright & Lodwick, 1989).

This research aims to examine the lived experience of Aleta and Douglas to better understand research student experience and identity development. Specifically, it asks:

1. What are the experiences of research students in terms of research supervision and research training?
2. What are effective forms of support for research student education and development?
3. What strategies can students, supervisors, researcher development specialists, and the institution undertake to ensure positive research student experiences and researcher identities?

The research seeks to identify effective forms of support for research student education and development, and recommend strategies students, supervisors, researcher development specialists, and educational institutions can undertake to better ensure positive research student experiences and researcher identities. Identity theory, identity-trajectory theory, and the Community of Inquiry (CoI) framework are used as theoretical lenses to analyze and make sense of Aleta's research journey experiences. The CoI framework has seldom been applied to the postgraduate research experience space and so this research contributes new insights in terms of teaching presence, cognitive presence, and social presence in student researcher training and development.

Community of Inquiry Framework

The Community of Inquiry (CoI) by Garrison et al. (2000) is a valid theory and framework in higher education research (Caskurlu, 2018; Stenbom, 2018) to understand ways to build and sustain online learning experiences. Throughout two decades, the CoI has been applied in varied education contexts to promote collaborative meaning-making and reflective thinking in the design of blended and online learning instruction (Castellanos-Reyes, 2020; Garrison, 2022).

At the crux of the CoI framework are the educational experiences happening through the process of coconstructing and reconstructing knowledge by members of a learning community interacting through critical thinking, analysis, questioning, and challenging assumptions (Garrison & Arbaugh, 2007). Collaboration and reflection allow students to learn critically and meaningfully (Garrison & Cleveland-Innes, 2005) while the facilitation and instruction, although seen as shared roles among teachers and learners, are directed toward the fulfillment of learning goals. Therefore, within a successful community of inquiry, the social interactions are not ends in themselves; rather these become explicit processes for knowledge sharing and intellectual discourse to be sustained over a period of time toward high-level learning (Palloff & Pratt, 2007).

Within the CoI framework are the three elements or presences which make for active learning and productive online learning community building (Arbaugh et al., 2010). These elements are teaching presence, cognitive presence, and social presence. Teaching presence is "the design, facilitation, and direction of cognitive and social processes for the purpose of realizing personally meaningful and educationally worthwhile learning outcomes" (Anderson et al., 2001, p. 5). Cognitive presence is defined "as the extent to which learners are able to construct and confirm meaning through sustained reflection and discourse in a critical community of inquiry" (Garrison et al., 2001, p. 11). Social presence "is the ability of participants to identify with a group, communicate openly in a trusting environment, and develop personal and affective relationships progressively by way of projecting their individual personalities" (Garrison, 2017, p. 25). The intersections of these presences also afford enriching educational experiences, namely: setting the climate, selecting content, and supporting discourse to facilitate deep learning (Garrison et al., 2000; Swan & Ice, 2010).

Recently, the CoI elements and its intersections have been validated in the K-12 setting and with practical recommendation to examine and promote teacher self-reflection and learning community building among active members (Villanueva, 2021a). This was undertaken by Aleta in her dissertation, and hence it came naturally for her to use the CoI in examining her doctoral student experiences as she undertook most of her learning and consultations online as an externally based international student. This book is deemed fit to likewise examine doctoral student experiences through the intersections of the presences.

Identity and the Doctoral Research Journey

Research journeys have been well documented in higher education studies through the conceptual lens of identity. Given its broad application across disciplines, there is a mix of both allied and contending views on identity's definitions and dimensions (Vignoles 2011). One approach views identity as personally and developmentally constructed, rooted in internal structures such as cognition, behavior, and attitudes, while another considers identity as a by-product of social-cultural factors as well as historical contexts. For example, studies on teacher identity grounded on a personal and developmental perspective assert that teacher identity formation involves psychological processes and the factor of emotions (Akkerman & Meijer, 2011; Bukor, 2015; van Lankveld et al., 2017). On the other hand, studies on teacher identity based on a sociocultural perspective recognize identity as constructed from professional roles and functions as well as transitions and challenges brought about by workplace culture (Assaf, 2008; Levin & Hernandez, 2014; Pratt et al., 2006). Narratives of the hybridity and multiplicity of roles as well as tensions among teachers transitioning to a university-based profession are clear examples of this perspective (Beauchamp & Thomas, 2009; Carrillo & Baguley, 2011; Hökkä et al., 2012). This view therefore

Table 1 Key themes of this book in relation to identity

Key themes of the doctoral research journey	Identity intersections	Identity subconstructs
Research as an expression of the self	(i) A K-12 teacher identity and a doctoral research student identity	Personal identity and multiple identities
Research as a reflective practice	(ii) K-12 teacher-researcher identity and higher education professional identity	Hybrid identity Relational identity
Research as a rite of passage	(iii) Higher education academic identity and doctoral research student identity	Relational identity Shifting identity Collective identity
Research as learning community building Research as a collaborative act	(iv) An international on-campus student identity and online/external student identity	Scholarly identity Academic identity Collaborative research identity

affirms identity as contextually driven (Côté & Levine, 2002). In the doctoral education research literature, Castelló et al. (2021) presented a continuum where socially constructed meanings of identity fall under the interpretivist/constructivist meta-theory. This book views identity as such and therefore leans toward a postpositivist paradigm.

On the one hand, the doctoral research journey in this book acknowledges the sociocultural stance of identity as neither transfixed nor a linear process but rather what can be characterized as rhizomatic (Guerin, 2013; Taylor et al., 2011). Therefore, we see identity as rather evolving, layered and shifting as the story unpeels the varied experiences in place and in time. This book defines identity as embedded in "stories that people tell themselves and others about who they are, and who they are not, as well as who and how they would like to/should be" (Yuval-Davis, 2010, p. 266). The book acknowledges that the act of storytelling is agentive as new meanings on identity are constructed in the process of the telling and between the teller and the told. The story unfolds within the cultural context of the academe, both in the Philippines and Australian university settings and therefore is not bereft of influences from external factors.

On the other hand, the doctoral journey may also be understood along the intersections of identities as experienced in the span of Aleta's PhD v.1.0 and v.2.0. The autoethnographic account touches on these intersections, with varied notions of identity reflected in the story. An initial view of identity subconstructs which this story uncovers is found in Table 1.

These intersections of identities within the doctoral student journey affirm the notion of the multiplicity in one's identity and as constructed throughout time. As with most doctoral research experiences, the journey was marked by inner struggles, tensions, and constraints as well as motivations and enablers. Navigating the journey entailed a mix of thinking hats to make sense of both the personal and professional life experiences alongside the scholarly experiences which at certain times, resulted in conflicting identities giving way to a quest for unity in these identities. The act of storytelling from the backend and initial autoethnographic writing raised teacher identity (Beauchamp & Thomas, 2009; Carrillo & Baguley, 2011; van Lankveld et al., 2017) as the core of Aleta's PhD v.1.0 which fueled the initial doctoral quests, hence the birth of an alternate identity—that of a scholar. Her imagined future was for the doctoral degree to be a springboard into a more stable teacher-leader identity through improved school leadership and self-enhancement (Gregg et al., 2011). The result, however, was a shift to teacher-educator identity (Swennen et al., 2010).

As such, Aleta's quest for equilibrium, amid uncertainty, as an academic in higher education was rooted in the painful yet insightful experiences embodied in her PhD v.1.0. The failure to complete PhD v.1.0 interrupted her scholarly identity development until she transitioned from a K-12 classroom educator to a member of the academe. The pathway for her scholarly identity to continue evolving (Baker & Lattuca, 2010; Ching, 2021) was expressed in research interests straddled between K-12 and higher education scholarly works which came fully into fruition in her PhD v.2.0 journey.

Unpacking the doctoral research journey solely through the subconstructs of identity summarized above is problematic as it results in a linear or fragmented story, which may not attain the goal of having concrete recommendations for a more in-depth understanding of the doctoral student experience and meaningful student support. In truth, the accounts in this book are multi-layered. To enable connectedness in the layered accounts in the chapters, the construct of identity-trajectory is used to reflect on and discuss the doctoral student experience. For example, it can be said that at some point in both Douglas' and Aleta's life, the doctoral research student and academic-professional experiences and corresponding identities are intertwined. Perhaps even, at some points, these identities are melded although forged in completely different settings. Likewise, the use of the terms 'scholarly identity', 'researcher identity', and 'academic identity' have evolved in this book and are applied at different points across the chapters. Therefore, the identity-trajectory framework proposed by McAlpine and Amundsen (2009, 2018) is the most suitable lens to understand nuances and variabilities in doctoral student journeys. The next section further defines identity terminologies utilized in this book and more importantly discusses and justifies why identity-trajectory was a fitting framework for different aspects of this work.

Scholarly Identity, Researcher Identity, and Academic Identity

With Douglas including Aleta in the Research and Writing League (RWL) and the International Doctoral Education Research Network (IDERN), came the opportunity to connect with others engaged either in their research study or research into

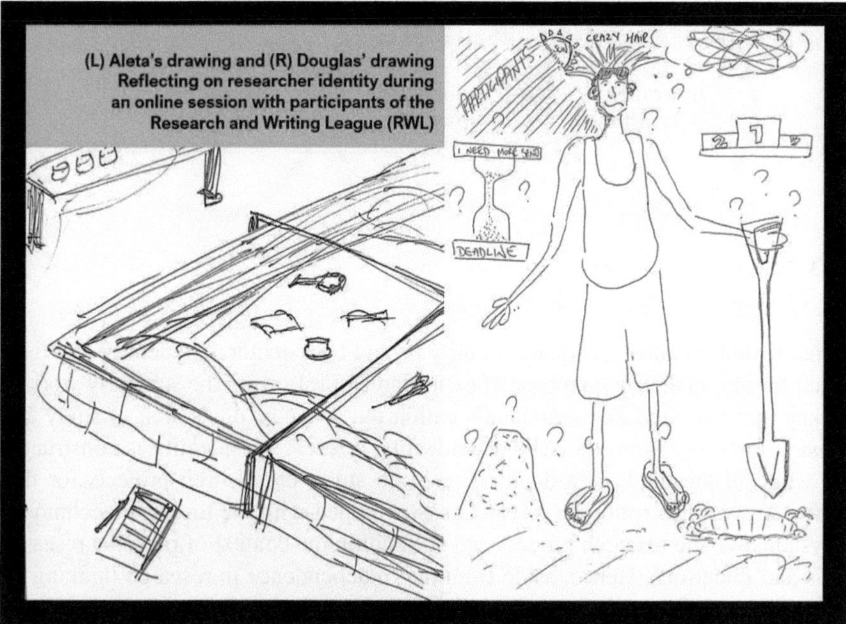

Fig. 2 Drawings by Aleta and Douglas while reflecting on researcher identity

doctoral education and a body of work highlighting doctoral writing and pedagogies, researcher identity, and academic identity construction. In the RWL online sessions, we reflected collaboratively on our researcher identities (Fig. 2).

Some of the guide questions to help us reflect on our drawings included: What important elements of researcher identity are present in the drawing? How does this researcher compare to your own perceived identity as a researcher? For Aleta, the reflection went this way:

> …my own drawing to represent research and my researcher identity is a sandbox turned into an actual archeological dig. I enjoy the 'play' and daydreaming involved while conceptualizing the research or putting a proposal together. I like tools/apps to play with but then I have to remind myself that at some point, I need to be systematic and really focus on what needs to be put on the table of finds or the actual artefacts (data for presentation and analysis) and for proper documentation. Whether the artefacts will be on display or not is not my call. I need not concern myself with what my viewer will make out if it. But if you have done the process with great care and hard work, it is bound to be remembered or even valued by those who can make meaning out of it.

After a failed PhD v.1.0, Aleta was back on track in her PhD v.2.0 and this time seeing herself as operating on a 'researcher identity' evolving out of a 'scholarly identity'. Inouye and McAlpine (2017) indicated scholarly identity as "self-confidence, independence in research thinking, positioning the self in relation to others" (p. 2). This book maintains the initial researcher self in relation to others takes place in

Fig. 3 Interconnectedness of Identity

an intertextual manner. Scholarly identity is held by a doctoral student or any individual for that matter in the phase of exploring and following the scholarly work or the key literature and key individuals within the scope of one's area of study and research interests. From the scholarly identity, a researcher identity is constructed and while in the thick of a doctoral research study or research projects for that matter. Around this time, the researcher is equipped with the tools and techniques to systematize the research process and still within the context of personal research goals and intentions. Hence, aside from the 'independence in research thinking' is the acquisition of interdisciplinary skills and habits of mind to bravely undertake an independent study or collaborative research project. The researcher identity feeds into one's academic identity formation especially for those engaged in higher education fulfilling functions in teaching, research, and public service which contribute to institutional building and the industry (Fig. 3).

Academic identity evolves just as well and enacted through the navigation of "discourses of knowledge and master narratives within the academy" (Giampapa, 2011, p. 135) to include roles and opportunities whether chosen or prescribed within the university as an institution. Key to these identity definitions is the setting/context where these identities are shaped and played out. For example, a K-12 educator would hold a teacher identity versus a higher education instructor, but both may initially hold a scholarly identity as both may engage in scholarly work. However, those involved in a higher education work setting will most likely identify with 'academic identity' as she/he moves on the path of becoming an academic responsible for undertaking research projects and administrative roles required of being a member of the academe. As such, for Douglas the reflection on his researcher identity drawing was as follows:

> …my drawing represents the research process and resultant identity as a day at the beach. Researcher identity is conceived of as a somewhat crazy process where there is too much sand and not enough time. The stressors of producing more research in less time and with less resources become overwhelming and result in spinning ideas, crazy hair and a less than enjoyable day at the beach moving sand. This is offset by a researcher perspective that seeks to ignore neoliberal demands to achieve more with less, and instead focus on the underlying 'real' motivation to conduct research. This is to achieve outcomes that benefit participants, and society, in tangible ways. Finding time to achieve this, and develop this type of researcher identity, among competing priorities can be difficult.

Hence, as illustrated in the elements found in Douglas drawing (Fig. 2), the struggle to maintain protected time for the nurturance of one's 'researcher identity' was evident.

Identity-Trajectory in Doctoral Student Research

Prior studies on doctoral research experiences focus on a sociocultural perspective of identity (Inouye & McAlpine, 2019) and presume that identity formation of researchers is rooted on their doctoral study (Ching, 2021). While undertaking the PhD and post-PhD, identity is enhanced with the acquisition of graduate attributes (Platow, 2012), leadership skills (Wilkes & Mohan, 2008), and recognition in the academe where shared values among like-minded scholars or work peers are experienced (Winter, 2009). However, recent studies indicate that this view does not fully consider the wider contexts by which doctoral research students construct their identities (McAlpine et al., 2014). Drawing from the earlier works on identity by Gee (2000) and Sfard and Prusak (2005), McAlpine (2012a) proposes identity-trajectory as an alternate perspective which views the doctoral student's life goals and scholarly work as interconnected and evolving throughout time. It recognizes academic identity as embedded in their day-to-day lives as real persons with past experiences, as well as relationships and accountabilities (McAlpine & Amundsen, 2009).

Within the sphere of doctoral research and academic work are interconnected strands, explained by McAlpine (2012a) as follows:

- Intellectual—written and oral contributions to the field leading to recognition;
- Networking—present and past relationships which serve as resources as well as carry responsibilities and;
- Institutional—organizational responsibilities and resources (p. 39).

The networking strand, in the context of doctoral research, may take place through interpersonal and intertextual relationships (McAlpine et al., 2014). Doctoral students seek support from family and friends while building on collegial ties through their collaborative networks, nationally and internationally. This interpersonal networking can coincide with the students' scholarly body of works during their doctoral journey, considered as intertextual networking. This kind of networking entails sustained thinking, reading, and conversing on the literature of their chosen discipline (McAlpine, 2012b) which they retain on their journey into academic life.

With the networking strand is the intellectual strand of identity-trajectory demonstrated by the fine-tuning of scholarly thinking and broadening of theoretical knowledge and research interests. These are represented by concrete intellectual outcomes in the form of papers and published works (McAlpine, 2012b), some of which may be intentionally targeted as doctoral writing milestones at different points of the doctoral journey.

Key to the identity-trajectory perspective is the construct of agency defined as "efforts to be intentional, to plan, to construct a way forward given constraints

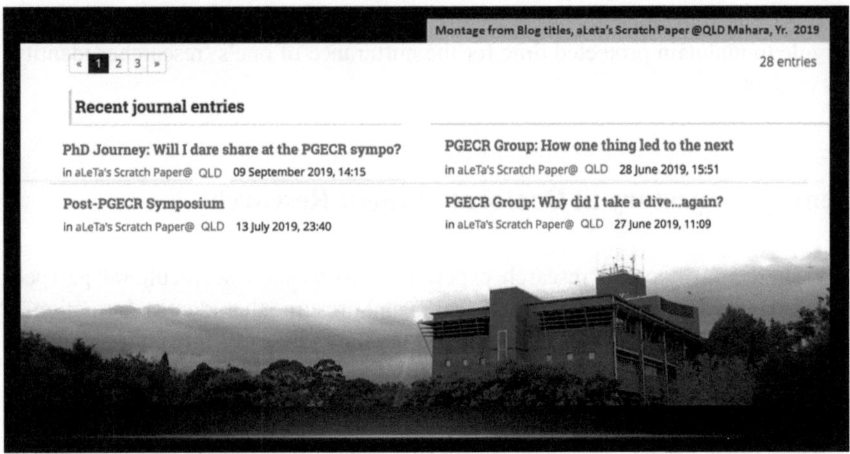

Fig. 4 Montage of Aleta's Journal Entry Titles from an ePortfolio. *Note.* Adapted from Villanueva (2021b), "Becoming part of a collaborative learning culture at a QLD university", presentation at a CoPRS meeting

(whether expected or unexpected)—though not always successfully" (McAlpine, 2012a, p. 39). Degrees of agency among individuals vary in these strands, depending on their engagement while immersed in their doctoral studies and academic work demands. For example, an academic in a higher education institution who is also in pursuit of doctoral studies may be able to tap into a wider set of resources through existing interpersonal networks and institutional support.

It has also been reported that early career doctoral students experience supervisor feedback and relationship building differently resulting in variations to the growth of their scholarly identity defined by Inouye and McAlpine (2017) as the "sense of confidence, scholarly independence in thinking, and positioning in relation to others and academic identity" (p. ii). Supervisor feedback is dealt with differently by doctoral students across the elements of identity-trajectory. These likewise signify nuances in their sense of agency as well as the development of their scholarly identity. Selected chapters of this book not only highlight the role of the research supervisors and mentors in reaffirming Aleta's scholarly identity and intellectual contribution but also the valuable role third space academics such as researcher development specialists and Learning Advisors play, in helping students cope with the rudiments of scholarly writing and publishing as well as managing the emotions and expectations which go with these processes.

The doctoral journey is not only about the 'what'—the significant and original contribution made to the field, but also the 'how'—the rigorous act of academic reading and writing, partly shaped by sustained actual access to a variety of human, physical and material resources in support of the doctoral journey (McAlpine & Amundsen, 2012). These are representations of the institutional strand of identity-trajectory. Chapters 4 and 5 of this book cover a time in Aleta's PhD v.2.0 journey highlighting outcomes of her intentions to experience both online/off-campus and

Scratch Paper

aLeTa's evolving quests, confusions and equilibrium

Labels

AuthoEthno Experiment **(10)** Brainstorms **(16)** Buhay Binan **(10)** Collegial X-changes **(12)** CWTS ECOTrack **(2)** Dissertation **(11)** Dragon Slaying **(16)** Friendly Advise ;) **(2)** Inquiry Paper **(1)** Mauro et Miranda **(12)** Musings **(45)** On Quali Research **(23)** Prof Life **(22)** Research as a Personal Act **(9)** Research as a Purifying Act **(2)** Research as my Reflective Practice **(19)** Research on Online Teaching at WizIQ **(26)** Sense of Community Study **(14)** Social Presence **(1)** Teaching Presence **(6)** Theses 2B **(33)** Thoughts on WizIQ **(6)** Toowoomba Sojourn **(6)** UPOU Community Site **(4)**

Blog Archive

2022 **(1)**
2021 **(3)**
2020 **(21)**
2019 **(16)**
2018 **(1)**
2017 **(10)**
2016 **(3)**
2015 **(11)**
2014 **(17)**
2013 **(9)**
2012 **(19)**
2011 **(56)**
2010 **(30)**
2009 **(12)**

aLeTa's Scratch Paper @QLD Mahara ePortfolio

A record of aLeTa's journey through her research project ... only @QLD with more pathways to get somewhere

Fig. 5 Montage of Labels and Captions from Aleta's Two Blog Sites. *Note*. Adapted from Villanueva (2019/2021a, 2021b) "Research journey: A tale from the backend" (https://fed.upou.edu.ph/research-journeys-2/)

on-campus doctoral student life. An increase in her digital artifacts, mainly blogs and social media posts during on-campus study, demonstrates how on-campus opportunities were maximized, an indication of the institutional strand's influence on her academic identity development. Another set of blogs was created in the university's eportfolio platform (Fig. 4) while still maintaining the title Scratch Paper she has used since 2009 (Fig. 5).

The journal entries served to document looking back while making steps forward as she progressed in her research study and mainly while on-campus. This continued as she transitioned to her home country to complete her dissertation and at the onset of the COVID-19 pandemic.

Initial identity-trajectory studies relied heavily on narratives as a methodology and longitudinal studies following early career doctoral students until their post-PhD years. These studies perceive individuals as change agents within their varied contexts, engaged in the ongoing process of identity construction, pre-, during, and post, doctoral studies. We see identity-trajectory as likewise befitting in understanding doctoral research students' lives whose stories and contexts bring to the fore their intentionality amid the unusual and unique circumstances spanning early career to mid-career and post-PhD years. Biographical accounts demonstrating personal and work transitions are also valued especially since these are embedded in the autoethnographic writing of this book.

How We Did It

This book takes a collaborative autoethnographic approach, making use of narrative analysis (e.g., narratology), to reflect on the student research journey from the perspective of a recent Doctor of Philosophy graduate and a researcher development specialist. This approach allows the researchers to provide a personal narrative account while still individually and collaboratively extracting meaningful learnings for analysis and dissemination. It is through these deep dives into the data that significant and nuanced aspects of the research student journey can be identified and interrogated in a way that balances subjective storytelling with objective and reliable research methods.

Autoethnography is the study of cultural issues through the personal experiences and subjective self-reflection of the individual researcher or researchers (Adams et al., 2022; Chang et al., 2016). The benefits of this qualitative research method include '(1) disrupting norms of research practice and representation; (2) working from insider knowledge; (3) maneuvering through pain, confusion, anger, and uncertainty and making life better; (4) breaking silence/(re)claiming voice and "writing to right" (Bolen, 2012); and (5) making work accessible' (Holman Jones et al., 2016, p. 32). Many of these benefits are the result of the reflexive, subjective, and narrative approach of autoethnography which allow the research to be carried out in ways that account for the researcher's voice and facilitate more personal control over the narrative and related analysis. The closeness and personal investment in recounting and making sense of personal experience mean that autoethnography provides a powerful lens for the researcher/s to understand their own experience and reflect on what this might mean for 'others' in similar cultural contexts. In the field of doctoral education, these advantages have been demonstrated in autoethnographic investigations into doctoral milestones (Bartlett & Eacersall, 2019), reflections on the doctoral thesis (Lake, 2015), and doctoral wellbeing (Pretorius & Cutri, 2019).

The strength of autoethnography's focus on the subjective gaze can also be a limitation (Chang, 2016). This is especially acute in the case of individual autoethnography, which involves only one research participant—the researcher themselves. With a single researcher focusing on their own narratives there is a risk that the view becomes too narrow, and the research overemphasizes a single perspective (Chang, 2016). Although it could be argued that these narratives often involve artifacts and interactions that incorporate other people's perspectives (as is the case with all qualitative research), autoethnography's focus on subjective reflection can mean that this limitation is more acute. To reduce this limitation, while still taking advantage of the subjective strengths of an autoethnographic approach, this research uses a collaborative autoethnographic method.

Collaborative autoethnography involves two people, or more, reflecting and analyzing on their own, as well as each other's, experiences (Chang, 2016). This approach reduces the insular nature of individual autoethnography, as additional researchers increase the number of perspectives and add additional levels of objectivity (Lapadat, 2017). This results in improved research rigor and reliability. The benefits of collaborating include "(1) collective exploration of researcher subjectivity; (2) power-sharing among researcher-participants; (3) efficiency and enrichment in the research process; (4) deeper learning about self and other; and (5) community building" (Chang et al., 2016, p. 25). Many of these benefits were realized during this research.

Collaborative autoethnography also has limitations. There are several issues to consider when discussing the limitations of collaborative autoethnography. These include the logistics of managing the team, ethical considerations regarding data ownership, power differentials between collaborators, the prevalence of miscommunication, particular perspectives dominating others, and the importance of establishing trusting relationships (Chang, 2016; Chang et al., 2016; Lapadat, 2017). These issues add a level of complexity to collaborative autoethnography, especially when compared to individual autoethnography. This research took a considered and balanced approach to account for these complexities and ensure consensus without one voice dominating another. This was aided by the high levels of mutual respect and trust developed by the researchers through prior collaborations and the experience of a shared research journey.

Working collaboratively on the autoethnography involved Aleta first writing parts of the narrative and analysis and Douglas then adding written analysis and self-reflection. The writing, incorporating both distinct voices, could then be discussed to reach a consensus or negotiate a means to represent both perspectives. This iterative approach of writing first, discussing later, and then rewriting meant that the original voices were clear and present thus limiting the potential for one voice to dominate another but also allowed for negotiation and discussion to reach a consensus on the overall direction of the work. This multifaceted and multi-staged approach limited the privileging or exclusion of one voice over the other, encouraged open and honest communication, and capitalized on established relationships of trust. It also assisted to balance and integrate the narrative and analytical elements of the work.

Approaches to autoethnography are described as existing on a continuum with one end accentuating the autobiographical emotive narrative and the other placing more emphasis on ethnographical analysis (Chang et al., 2016). This project took a story driven but analytical approach in that the emphasis was on analyzing stories of the self from an ethnographical perspective to understand these particular experiences. The focus is the story of Aleta's doctoral journey but with analysis provided at key points along the way. This analysis draws on relevant academic literature, curation of, and reflection on, Aleta's and Douglas' ethnographical artifacts (e.g., blogs, email correspondence, research training sessions, doctoral writing feedback consultations, and collaborative reflections through a shared writing group), experiences of doctoral study, and other research students' journeys.

It is important that autoethnographic research considers issues of ethical research conduct when undertaking self-reflection and analysis of data (Edwards, 2021) which may also involve third parties. This research followed ethical guidelines and gained ethical approval from both Aleta's and Douglas' respective institutions. Part of this process involved gaining consent from and/or anonymizing participants within the narrative account. Pseudonyms are used throughout the work and are reflective of those already used by Aleta in her blogs and personal writings. These mostly relate to superheroes she found resembled the personal qualities of the individuals involved. For example, Douglas was referred to as Bruce Wayne and/or Batman, and others as Superfriends.

The process of collating and reflecting on Aleta's personal writings was recursive and entailed the following:

(1) Writing an initial storyline based on pre-existing themes as found in blog labels;
(2) Identifying key events in the narrative;
(3) Curating personal blog entries from pre-existing themes;
(4) Reexamining other personal blog entries under labels related to research and academic writing (Figs. 4 and 5);
(5) Developing new themes aligned with the narrative;
(6) Searching for email correspondence aligned with blog entries and key events;
(7) Weaving blog excerpts to build on the key events of the storyline;
(8) Inserting additional diary entries/short reflections;
(9) Reviewing parts of the narrative;
(10) Collaborative reflection on research identity.

Throughout the book chapters are excerpts from blog posts and montages of social media images or screenshots from personal mobile phone pictures and other stored files. Some were adapted from Aleta's original online posts and work files. The dates and chosen paragraphs or statements have been included, being careful also to place the de-identified versions in the book.

Aleta: Writing the blog allowed feelings and thoughts of my PhD v.1.0 to surface which had been buried deep down. These have been blogged about at different points since 2009 at "Scratch Paper, Aleta's evolving quests, ideas and equilibrium", at *thisisgettingitchy.blogspot.com.* The site uniform resource locator (URL) is a pun on my need to relieve myself from the brain itchiness resulting from a clutter of thoughts, ideas, inner speeches, worries, and reveries amid making sense of multiple, intersecting, and sometimes conflicting identities. The virtual blogspace became a vehicle to declutter thoughts and hence served as an online diary at the tip of my fingers. As I switched among varied roles in the realm of education, blogging became a good way to cope with an academic, creative, and hectic everyday life. I also found safety in my blogspace where I am not necessarily being 'followed' nor seen automatically by 'friends' and so the anonymity provided a sense of comfort.

Blogging and Identity Building

Blogging and research journeys go hand in hand within higher education environments (Bennett & Folley, 2014). Beyond a daily record of the self, however, Gurak and Antonijevic (2008) explain that "blogs illustrate the fusion of key elements of human desire—to express one's identity, create community, structure one's past and present experiences—with the main technological features of twenty-first century digital communication" (p. 60). Blogging involves "rewriting of the self" (Gurak & Antonijevic, 2008, p. 65), putting focus on the construction, deconstruction, and reconstruction of the individual. In so doing, multiple facets of one's identity are embodied in the writing and process of meaning-making. In Aleta's case, blogging on personal and professional life experiences was undertaken alongside her doctoral research journey. Aleta's process of blogging is likened to a self-study into educational practices (Coia & Taylor, 2005; Hamilton et al., 2008) but undertaken as reflections in an online format. The blogs with corresponding titles and labels (see Fig. 5) can be deemed as Aleta's conversation with the self as a means to sort out her ongoing thoughts and feelings, in order to provide centering and clarity in her higher education practices amid multiple roles and intersecting identities. Hence, the act of blogging served as a filtering device or a form of self-enhancement and self-assessment, defined by Gregg et al. (2011) as "the former denotes the drive to see oneself positively, the latter, the drive to see oneself accurately" (p. 305).

McAlpine and Amundsen (2009) acknowledge the act of storytelling as part of identity building but in a manner that highlights the doctoral student's learning and sense of agency. Although she was not aware at the time, Aleta's sharing of curated blogs to Douglas during her PhD v.2.0, in preparation for a graduate research symposium, was part of her scholarly identity building process. The storytelling and retelling from the blog demonstrate Aleta's agency during the critical stages of her dissertation writing phase and her transition back to her workplace during the pandemic. Collaborative reflection and analysis were undertaken with special emphasis on the construction/deconstruction of identities and an identity-trajectory lens. Each chapter discusses Aleta's story from this perspective, and intertwined with her autoethnographic voice is Douglas', as well as their collaborative experience. Given the nature of the personal data and reflections, the findings are presented as narratives of lived experiences according to Browning's (2009) narratology. The latter part of the narrative resulted in layered accounts (Boylorn & Orbe, 2014) as the action-reflection became more closely intertwined during the dissertation writing phases and Aleta's transition back to her academic workplace.

What We Found

The story discusses the following themes: the doctoral research journey as an expression of the self; a reflective act; a rite of passage; a learning community building; and a collaborative act. In examining these themes, the research highlights the importance of the self, and significant others, in the research journey. As discussed in Chap. 1 and Chap. 2, the student's past experiences and sense of self can impact on their choice of research topic and its subsequent conceptualization. This investment of self in the topic can be an important motivating factor in research study but can also lead to topics where the personal investment clouds the student's judgment in developing a viable and timely project. Research as a reflective practice means that reflection on the literature, workplace learning, the student's current circumstances, topic, and motivations for pursuing it can lead to further enhancement and modifications of the project intertwined with identity transformation. Research as a rite of passage is covered in Chap. 3 where the cognitive and emotional challenges of research are outlined. This chapter demonstrates the topic development and especially personal researcher identity growth that can occur through overcoming research challenges, and that supervisory and additional supports outside of the supervisory team are vital to ensure positive research experiences during these times. Research as a collaborative act is discussed in Chap. 4—'Research as learning community building' and Chap. 5—'Research as a collaborative relationship'. In Chap. 4, social presence, teaching presence, and cognitive presence from the CoI framework are shown to be important elements in the development of positive research cultures for the support of student researchers and their identities. The role of additional supports outside of the supervisory team in developing these cultures is discussed as a means of improving student experience. Chapter 5 focuses on collaborative relationships especially in terms of trust and respect during the writing phases of the research student journey. Here, self-determination theory is put forward as an approach to ensure positive collaborations for the provision of writing feedback and other aspects of student research relationships.

The result of this collaborative autoethnographic process is a rich account of the highs and lows of the student research journey accompanied by insightful analysis and meaning-making. The book makes an original and significant contribution to the use of narratives in identity-trajectory research, but as evidenced by blogging and other digital artifacts, and strengthened using collaborative autoethnography as methodology. This has led to a deeper understanding of the self and our experiences as research student, early career researcher, and researcher development specialist and a broader cultural understanding of our interactions with significant stakeholders in the student research journey. These insights into student experience make a significant contribution to research student training and development and can be used for broader consideration, research, and application. This work contributes to the research student experience literature in the areas of project conceptualization, identity development, supervisor training, and collaborative research relationship building and benefits research students, supervisors, researcher development specialists, administrative staff, higher education institutions, and research training policy. Our insights and recommendations foster positive research cultures that limit damaging experiences and improve research experience not only for those experiencing difficulties but for research students more broadly. These types of research cultures support student success including successful completion, and research outputs, and a more enjoyable journey, leading to positive effects on student wellbeing and identity development. We hope this book resonates with, and sustains, those who experience the journey as research students themselves and assists those who share in the journey—the research supervisors, university leaders, the policy makers, the administrators, the library staff, and the research training and development providers. It is hoped that by using this experience-rich, more subjective approach that those on their own journey, those contemplating starting the journey, and those supporting the research journey will empathize and reflect on their own experiences and find hope and direction in the autoethnographic account provided.

References

Adams, T. E., Holman Jones, S. L., & Ellis, C. (2022). *Handbook of autoethnography* (2nd ed.). Routledge. https://doi.org/10.4324/9780429431760

Akkerman, S. F., & Meijer, P. C. (2011). A dialogical approach to conceptualizing teacher identity. *Teaching and Teacher Education, 27*(2), 308–319. https://doi.org/10.1016/j.tate.2010.08.013

Anderson, T., Rourke, L., Garrison, D. R., & Archer, W. (2001). Assessing teaching presence in a computer conferencing context. *Journal of Asychronous Learning Networks, 5*(2), 1–17. https://doi.org/10.24059/olj.v5i2.1875

Arbaugh, J. B. (2001). How instructor immediacy behaviors affect student satisfaction and learning in web-based courses. *Business Communication Quarterly, 64*(4), 42–54. https://doi.org/10.1177/108056990106400405

Arbaugh, J. B., Bangert, A., & Cleveland-Innes, M. (2010). Subject matter effects and the community of inquiry (COI) framework: An exploratory study. *The Internet and Higher Education, 13*(1), 37–44. https://doi.org/10.1016/j.iheduc.2009.10.006

Assaf, L. C. (2008). Professional identity of a reading teacher: Responding to high-stakes testing pressures. *Teachers and Teaching, 14*(3), 239–252. https://doi.org/10.1080/13540600802006137

Baker, V. L., & Lattuca, L. R. (2010). Developmental networks and learning: Toward an interdisciplinary perspective on identity development during doctoral study. *Studies in Higher Education, 35*(7), 807–827. https://doi.org/10.1080/03075070903501887

Bartlett, C. L., & Eacersall, D. C. (2019). Confirmation of candidature: An autoethnographic reflection from the dual identities of student and research administrator. In T. M. Machin, M. Clara, & P. A. Danaher (Eds.), *Traversing the doctorate* (pp. 29–56). Palgrave Macmillan.

Beasy, K., Emery, S., & Crawford, J. (2021). Drowning in the shallows: An Australian study of the PhD experience of wellbeing. *Teaching in Higher Education, 26*(4), 602–618. https://doi.org/10.1080/13562517.2019.1669014

Beauchamp, C., & Thomas, L. (2009). Understanding teacher identity: An overview of issues in the literature and implications for teacher education. *Cambridge Journal of Education, 39*(2), 175–189. https://doi.org/10.1080/03057640902902252

Bennett, E. & Folley, S. (2014) A tale of two doctoral students: social media tools and hybridised identities. *Research in Learning Technology, 22*, 23791. http://eprints.hud.ac.uk/id/eprint/20383/

Bolen, D. M. (2012). Toward an applied communication relational inqueery: Autoethnography, co-constructed narrative, and relational futures. https://digitalcommons.wayne.edu/oa_dissertations/531/

Boylorn, R. M., & Orbe, M. P. (Eds.). (2014). *Critical autoethnography: Intersecting cultural identities in everyday life* (1st ed.). Routledge. https://doi.org/10.4324/9781315431253

Bukor, E. (2015). Exploring teacher identity from a holistic perspective: Reconstructing and reconnecting personal and professional selves. *Teachers and Teaching, 21*(3), 305–327. https://doi.org/10.1080/13540602.2014.953818

Browning, L. (2009). Narrative and narratology. *Encyclopedia of Communication Theory, 2,* 673–677.

Brownlow, C., Eacersall, D., Nelson, C. W., Parsons-Smith, R. L., & Terry, P. C. (2022). Risks to mental health of higher degree by research (HDR) students during a global pandemic. *PLoS ONE, 17*(12), e0279698. https://doi.org/10.1371/journal.pone.0279698

Carniel, J., Hickey, A., Southey, K., Brömdal, A., Crowley-Cyr, L., Eacersall, D., Farmer, W., Gehrmann, R., Machin, T., & Pillay, Y. (2022). The ethics review and the humanities and social sciences: Disciplinary distinctions in ethics review processes. *Research Ethics, 19*(2), 139–156. https://doi.org/10.1177/17470161221147202

Carrillo, C., & Baguley, M. (2011). From school teacher to university lecturer: Illuminating the journey from the classroom to the university for two arts educators. *Teaching and Teacher Education, 27*(1), 62–72. https://doi.org/10.1016/j.tate.2010.07.003

Carter, S., Blumenstein, M., & Cook, C. (2013). Different for women? The challenges of doctoral studies. *Teaching in Higher Education, 18*(4), 339–351. https://doi.org/10.1080/13562517.2012.719159

Caskurlu, S. (2018). Confirming the subdimensions of teaching, social, and cognitive presences: A construct validity study. *Internet and Higher Education, 39,* 1–12. https://doi.org/10.1016/j.iheduc.2018.05.002

Castellanos-Reyes, D. (2020). 20 years of the community of inquiry framework. *TechTrends,* 1-4. https://doi.org/10.1007/s11528-020-00491-7

Castelló, M., McAlpine, L., Sala-Bubaré, A., Inouye, K., & Skakni, I. (2021). What perspectives underlie 'researcher identity'? A review of two decades of empirical studies. *Higher Education, 81,* 567–590. https://doi.org/10.1007/s10734-020-00557-8

Chang, H. (2016). Individual and collaborative autoethnography as method. In S. L. Holman Jones, T. E. Adams, & C. Ellis (Eds.), *Handbook of autoethnography* (pp. 107–122). Routledge.

Chang, H., Hernandez, K. A. C., & Ngunjiri, F. W. (2016). Collaborative autoethnography. *Routledge.* https://doi.org/10.4324/9781315432137

Ching, G. S. (2021). Academic identity and communities of practice: Narratives of social science academics career decisions in Taiwan. *Education Sciences, 11,* 388. https://doi.org/10.3390/educsci11080388

Coffman, K., Putman, P., Adkisson, A., Kriner, B., & Monaghan, C. (2016). Waiting for the expert to arrive: Using a community of practice to develop the scholarly identity of doctoral students. *International Journal of Teaching and Learning in Higher Education, 28*(1), 30–37. https://files.eric.ed.gov/fulltext/EJ1106332.pdf

Coia, L. & Taylor, M. (2005). From the inside out and the outside in. In C. Klosnik, C. Beck, A. R. Freese & A. P. Samaras (Eds.), *Making a difference in teacher education through self-study. Self-study of teaching and teacher education practices* (vol. 2). Springer. https://doi.org/10.1007/1-4020-3528-4_2

Côté, J. E., & Levine, C. G. (2002). Identity formation, agency, and culture: A social psychological synthesis. *Psychology Press.* https://doi.org/10.4324/9781410612199

Eacersall, D. (2018). Quest for student success: An exploration of the academic skill needs of higher degree by research students at a regional university. University of Southern Queensland. https://research.usq.edu.au/item/q74y8

Edwards, J. (2021). Ethical autoethnography: Is it possible? *International Journal of Qualitative Methods, 20.* https://doi.org/10.1177/1609406921995306

Garrison, D. R. (2017). E-learning in the twenty-first century: A community of inquiry framework for research and practice. Routledge.

Garrison, D. R. (2022, May 6). Faculty development and the community of inquiry. *Community of Inquiry.* https://www.thecommunityofinquiry.org/editorial34

Garrison, D. R., Anderson, T., & Archer, W. (2000). Critical inquiry in a text-based environment: Computer conferencing in higher education. *The Internet and Higher Education, 2*(2/3), 87–105. https://doi.org/10.1016/S1096-7516(00)00016-6

Garrison, D. R., Anderson, T., & Archer, W. (2001). Critical thinking, cognitive presence, and computer conferencing in distance education. *American Journal of Distance Education, 15*(1), 7–23. https://doi.org/10.1080/08923640109527071

Garrison, D. R., & Arbaugh, J. B. (2007). Researching the community of inquiry framework: Review, issues, and future directions. *The Internet and Higher Education, 10*(3), 157–172. https://doi.org/10.1016/j.iheduc.2007.04.001

Garrison, D. R., & Cleveland-Innes, M. (2005). Facilitating cognitive presence in online learning: Interaction is not enough. *The American Journal of Distance Education, 19*(3), 133–148. https://doi.org/10.1207/s15389286ajde1903_2

Gee, J. (2000). Identity as an analytic lens for research in education. *Review of Research in Education, 25*(99), 125. https://www.jstor.org/stable/11673220

Giampapa, F. (2011). The politics of "being and becoming" a researcher: Identity, power, and negotiating the field. *Journal of Language, Identity & Education, 10*(3), 132–144. https://doi.org/10.1080/15348458.2011.585304

Gregg, A. P., Sedikides, C., & Gebauer, J. E. (2011). Dynamics of identity: Between self-enhancement and self-assessment. In *Handbook of identity theory and research* (pp. 305–327). Springer. https://doi.org/10.1007/978-1-4419-7988-9_14

Guerin, C. (2013). Rhizomatic research cultures, writing groups and academic researcher identities. *International Journal of Doctoral Studies, 8*, 137–150. http://ijds.org/Volume8/IJDSv8p137-150Guerin0400.pdf

Gurak, L. J., & Antonijevic, S. (2008). The psychology of blogging: You, me, and everyone in between. *American Behavioral Scientist, 52*(1), 60–68. https://doi.org/10.1177/0002764208321341

Guthrie, S., Lichten, C., van Belle, J., Ball, S., Knack, A., & Hofman, J. (2017). Understanding mental health in the research environment: A rapid evidence assessment. In *RAND Europe, Royal Society and the Wellcome Trust.* https://www.rand.org/pubs/research_reports/RR2022.html

Hamilton, M. H., Smith, L., & Worthington, K. (2008). Fitting the methodology with the research: An exploration of narrative, self-study and auto-ethnography. *Studying Teacher Education, 4*(1), 17–28. https://doi.org/10.1080/17425960801976321

Hickey, A., Davis, S., Farmer, W., Dawidowicz, J., Moloney, C., Lamont-Mills, A., Carniel, J., Pillay, Y., Akenson, D., Brömdal, A., Gehrmann, R., Mills, D., Kolbe-Alexander, T., Machin, T., Reich, S., Southey, K., Crowley-Cyr, L., Watanabe, T., Davenport, J., … Maxwell, J. (2022). Beyond criticism of ethics review boards: Strategies for engaging research communities and enhancing ethical review processes. *Journal of Academic Ethics, 20*(4), 549–567.

Hockey, J. (1994). New territory: Problems of adjusting to the first year of a social science PhD. *Studies in Higher Education, 19*(2), 177–190. https://doi.org/10.1080/03075079412331382027

Hökkä, P., Eteläpelto, A., & Rasku-Puttonen, H. (2012). The professional agency of teacher educators amid academic discourses. *Journal of Education for Teaching, 38*(1), 83–102. https://doi.org/10.1080/02607476.2012.643659

Holman Jones, S. L., Adams, T. E., & Ellis, C. (2016). Introduction: Coming to know autoethnography as more than a method. In S. L. Holman Jones, T. E. Adams, & C. Ellis (Eds.), *Handbook of autoethnography* (pp. 17–48). Routledge. https://doi.org/10.4324/9781315427812

Inouye, K. S., & McAlpine, L. (2017). Developing scholarly identity: Variation in agentive responses to supervisor feedback. *Journal of University Teaching & Learning Practice, 14*(2). https://ro.uow.edu.au/jutlp/vol14/iss2/3

Inouye, K., & McAlpine, L. (2019). Developing academic identity: A review of the literature on doctoral writing and feedback. *International Journal of Doctoral Studies, 14*, 1–31. https://doi.org/10.28945/4168

Koole, M., & Stack, S. (2016). Doctoral students' identity positioning in networked learning environments. *Distance Education, 37*(1), 41–59. https://doi.org/10.1080/01587919.2016.1153961

Lake, J. (2015). Autoethnography and reflective practice: Reconstructing the doctoral thesis experience. *Reflective Practice, 16*(5), 677–687. https://doi.org/10.1080/14623943.2015.1071247

Lapadat, J. C. (2017). Ethics in autoethnography and collaborative autoethnography. *Qualitative Inquiry, 23*(8), 589–603. https://doi.org/10.1177/1077800417704462

Levin, J. S., & Hernandez, V. M. (2014). Divided identity: Part-time faculty in public colleges and universities. *The Review of Higher Education 37*(4), 531–557. https://doi.org/10.1353/rhe.2014. 0033

McAlpine, L. (2012a). Identity trajectories: Doctoral journeys from past to present to future. *Australian Universities Review 54*(1), 38–46. https://doi.org/10.3316/ielapa.424355529639257

McAlpine, L. (2012b). Shining a light on doctoral reading: Implications for doctoral identities and pedagogies. *Innovations in Education and Teaching International, 49*(4), 351–361. https://doi. org/10.1080/14703297.2012.728875

McAlpine, L., & Amundsen, C. (2009). Identity and agency: Pleasures and collegiality among the challenges of the doctoral journey. *Studies in Continuing Education, 31*(2), 109–125. https:// doi.org/10.1080/01580370902927378

McAlpine, L., & Amundsen, C. (2018). *Identity-trajectories of early career researchers.* Palgrave Macmillan. https://doi.org/10.1057/978-1-349-95287-8

McAlpine, L., Amundsen, C., & Turner, G. (2014). Identity-trajectory: Reframing early career academic experience. *British Educational Research Journal, 40*(6), 952–969. https://doi.org/ 10.1002/berj.3123

Palloff, R., & Pratt, K. (2007). *Building online learning communities: Effective strategies for the virtual classroom* (2nd ed.). Jossey-Bass.

Pifer, M., & Baker, V. (2016). Stage-based challenges and strategies for support in doctoral education: A practical guide for students, faculty members, and program administrators. *International Journal of Doctoral Studies, 11*, 15–34. https://doi.org/10.1080/15283488.2016.1190729

Platow, M. J. (2012). PhD experience and subsequent outcomes: A look at self-perceptions of acquired graduate attributes and supervisor support. *Studies in Higher Education, 37*(1), 103–118. https://doi.org/10.1080/03075079.2010.501104

Pratt, M. G., Rockmann, K. W., & Kaufmann, J. B. (2006). Constructing professional identity: The role of work and identity learning cycles in the customization of identity among medical residents. *Academy of Management Journal, 49*(2), 235–262. https://doi.org/10.5465/amj.2006. 20786060

Pretorius, L. (2019). Prelude: The topic chooses the researcher. In L. Pretorius, L. Macaulay, & B. Cahusac de Caux (Eds.), *Wellbeing in doctoral education: Insights and guidance from the student experience* (pp. 3–8). Springer.

Pretorius, L., & Cutri, J. (2019). Autoethnography: Researching personal experiences. In *Wellbeing in doctoral education* (pp. 27–34). Springer. https://doi.org/10.1007/978-981-13-9302-0_4

Scott, H. and Takarangi M. K. T. (2019). Measuring PhD student's psychological well-being: Are we seeing the whole picture? *Student Success, 10*(3),14–24. https://doi.org/10.5204/ssj.v10i3. 1294

Sfard, A., & Prusak, A. (2005). Telling identities: In search of an analytic tool for investigating learning as a culturally shaped activity. *Educational Researcher, 34*(4), 14–22. https://doi.org/ 10.3102/0013189X034004014

Stenbom, S. (2018). A systematic review of the community of inquiry survey. *The Internet and Higher Education, 39*, 22–32. https://doi.org/10.1016/j.iheduc.2018.06.001

Sverdlik, A., Hall, N. C., McAlpine, L., & Hubbard, K. (2018). The PhD experience: A review of the factors influencing doctoral students' completion, achievement, and well-being. *International Journal of Doctoral Studies 13*, 361–388. https://doi.org/10.28945/4113

Swan, K., & Ice, P. (2010). The community of inquiry framework ten years later: Introduction to the special issue. *The Internet and Higher Education, 13*(1–2), 1–4. https://doi.org/10.1016/j. iheduc.2009.11.003

Swennen, S., Jones, K., & Volman, M. (2010). Teacher educators: Their identities, sub-identities and implications for professional development. *Professional Development in Education, 36*(1–2), 131–148. https://doi.org/10.1080/19415250903457893

Taylor, C. A., Downs, Y., Baker, R., & C. Gladson, C. (2011). "I did it my way': Voice, visuality and identity in doctoral students' reflexive video narratives on their doctoral research journeys. *International Journal of Research and Method in Education, 34* (2)193–210. https://doi.org/10. 1080/1743727X.2011.578818 van Lankveld, T., Schoonenboom, J., Volman, M., Croiset, G., & Beishuizen, J. (2017). Developing a teacher identity in the university context: A systematic review of the literature. *Higher Education Research & Development, 36*(2), 325–342. https://doi.org/10.1080/07294360.2016.1208154

Vignoles, V. L. (2011). Identity motives. In S. J. Schwartz, K. Luyckx, & V. L. Vignoles (Eds.), *Handbook of identity theory and research* (pp. 403–432). https://doi.org/10.1007/978-1-4419-7988-9_18

Villanueva, J. A. R. (2019, November 15). *Research journey: A tale from the backend.* [Paper presentation]. 24th Postgraduate and Early Career Research Symposium, University of Southern Queensland, Toowoomba, Australia.

Villanueva, J. A. R. (2021a). Teaching presence in K-12 blended learning classes under the alternative delivery mode. *International Journal on Open and Distance e-Learning, 7*(1), 31–52. https://ijodel.com/index.php/ijodel/article/view/33

Villanueva, J. A. R (2021b, August 31). *Becoming part of a collaborative learning culture at USQ.* [PowerPoint slides]. Research Supervisors Community of Practice Meeting. University of Southern Queensland

Wilkes, L. M., & Mohan, S. (2008). Nurses in the clinical area: Relevance of a PhD. *Collegian, 15*(4), 135–141. https://doi.org/10.1016/j.colegn.2008.05.001

Winter, R. (2009). Academic manager or managed academic? Academic identity schisms in higher education. *Journal of Higher Education Policy and Management, 31*(22), 121–131. https://doi.org/10.1080/13600800902825835

Wright, J., & Lodwick, R. (1989). The process of the PhD: A study of the first year of doctoral study. *Research Papers in Education, 4*(1), 22–56. https://doi.org/10.1080/0267152890040103

Yuval-Davis, N. (2010). Theorizing identity: Beyond the 'us' and 'them' dichotomy. *Patterns of Prejudice, 4*(3), 261–280. https://doi.org/10.1080/0031322X.2010.489736

Part I
Ph.D. Version 1.0 ~ A Tale from the Backend

Chapter 1
Battlefield 1.0

Abstract Developing a feasible and successful research project can be a difficult undertaking. In this chapter, we reflect on the experiences of research students in conceptualizing and solidifying a viable project. Analysis of these reflections identified several important issues for students, supervisors, and higher education providers to consider regarding research student training and development. These include personal investment in the topic and potential bias, discipline requirements, the need to make an original and significant contribution, and institutional and supervisory approaches to support the project development process. We conclude that institutional and supervisory support are important elements for student success. They can ensure that projects and researchers, especially those with a personal research agenda, are developed in ways that ensure the strengths of such an approach are realized while still aligning with discipline and program requirements.

Keywords Doctoral Education · Research student · Student experience · Student success · Researcher identity · Higher Degree by Research · HDR · Postgraduate Research · PGR · Original and significant contribution

BLOG POST: THE PERSONAL IS POLITICAL

FRIDAY, DECEMBER 31, 2010

While undertaking my doctoral studies, I wrote a paper in the first person for a class at my home university. I was cautioned against the use of 'I'. I found that troubling as most of the journal articles I connected with were written in first person. I wondered: how come they can, and I can't?

Now, at the tail-end of my doctoral coursework, I took a Qualitative methodology course with a colleague at my university of employment. I chanced upon this article which captured what I really meant. It came from a group of women doing a collaborative auto-ethnography... yes, there is such a thing!

Ngunjiri, F. W., Hernandez, K. C., & Chang, H. (2010). Living autoethnography: Connecting life and research [Editorial]. Journal of Research Practice, 6(1), Article E1. Retrieved from http://jrp.icaap.org/index.php/jrp/article/view/241/186

"Research is an extension of researchers' lives. Although most social scientists have been trained to guard against subjectivity (self-driven perspectives) and to separate self from

J. A. R. Villanueva and D. C. F. Eacersall, *Autoethnographic Reflections on a Research Journey*, SpringerBriefs in Education, https://doi.org/10.1007/978-981-99-4929-8_2

Fig. 1.1 Screenshot of Teacher Aleta and Teacher Vic of the Builders' School. *Note.* Adapted from Villanueva (2019/2021), "Research journey: A tale from the backend" (https://fed.upou.edu.ph/res earch-journeys-2/)

research activities, it is an impossible task. Scholarship is inextricably connected to self-personal interest, experience, and familiarity. Working together on this special issue provided an opportunity for us to candidly reflect on and dialogue about the motivations behind our scholarship. Not surprisingly, at the very onset our dissertation studies were anchored in our personal interests" (p. 2). (Villanueva, 2010)

Aleta: My doctoral research journey was born within the context of my personal battlefield of sorts. Battlefield 1.0 is a space I share with my husband, Teacher Vic with regards to the teaching profession. We both graduated from the top university of the country in the Philippines. We were fighting for our lives as teachers at a time when most of our relatives and teacher-friends had gone abroad to seek greener pastures. While these well-trained teachers in special education and reading education went to the United States or Canada, Teacher Vic and I (Fig. 1.1) held on to our shared passion for teaching in our home country, as well as shared views when it comes to politics and governance. Hence, we found more important reasons to stay put and contribute to our nation's development in our own special way as Filipino educators.

One of the reasons we stayed was to establish the Builders' School, a private coeducational multigrade school for preschool to Grade 7 children. This is one of the few progressive schools in the Philippines set up by a small group of teacher-leaders. These schools were established for our own children because we realized that our beliefs in education were not aligned with the traditional school system in our country. The schools we established attract families and children in search of more meaningful and personalized learning. Some of our students have difficulties coping within traditional school systems and our approach sought to align more with a progressive philosophy and eclectic teaching methods to address their learning

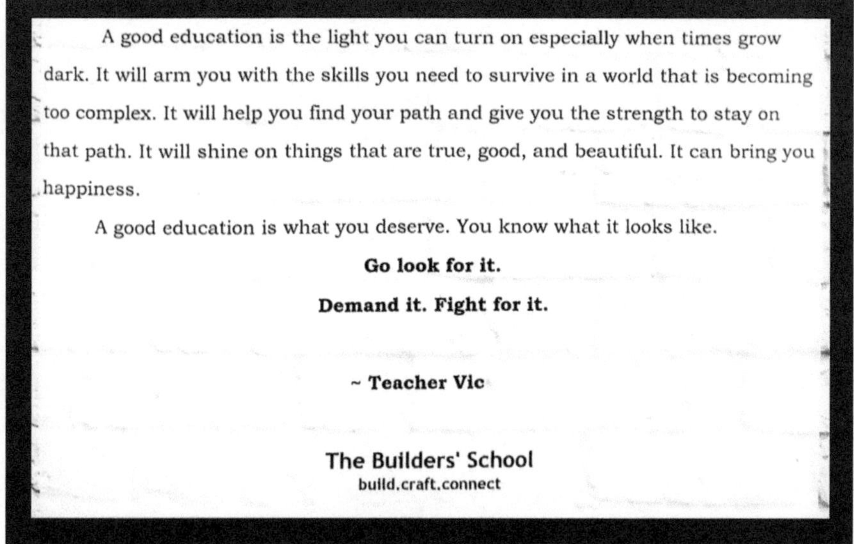

Fig. 1.2 A personal statement on education by Teacher Vic. *Note.* Adapted from "A Message to the Graduates" in The Blueprint, 2015 by The Builders' School, Inc. Reprinted with permission

needs. The vision we had for our school can be seen in an excerpt (Fig. 1.2) from my husband, Teacher Vic, who took on the role of School Director.

I became the Program Coordinator responsible for overseeing the development of our school curriculum and program direction. At this time, I was two years into my doctoral study in education with specialization in curriculum work. The doctoral program entailed more than 50 units of coursework which I undertook on a part-time basis. Through my courses, I made sense and codified our evolving progressive school philosophy and practices, and developed associated research interests. This led to my first stints into academic writing and conference presentations (Fig. 1.3). These research outputs involved educational ideas that began to form a potential thesis topic for my doctoral studies.

In my sixth year as a part-time to full-time doctoral student, I finally conceptualized a research topic proposal, with a running title: Curriculum Development of Social Studies in Philippine Progressive Schools and a set of objectives and questions (Fig. 1.4). I was interested in investigating the process and outcomes by which teacher-leaders and other schoolteachers codesign Social Studies as a core or key curriculum area in three progressive schools.

Prior to my actual research proposal presentation, my classmates and I did a mock panel presentation with faculty members present. A professor who was part of the mock panel expressed agreement with the research topic and even provided words of encouragement. A semester passed and then came the day for the actual topic presentation to a panel. I did not feel that nervous at that time, but I can only recall two distinct panel comments on my research topic presentation: (1) There was no

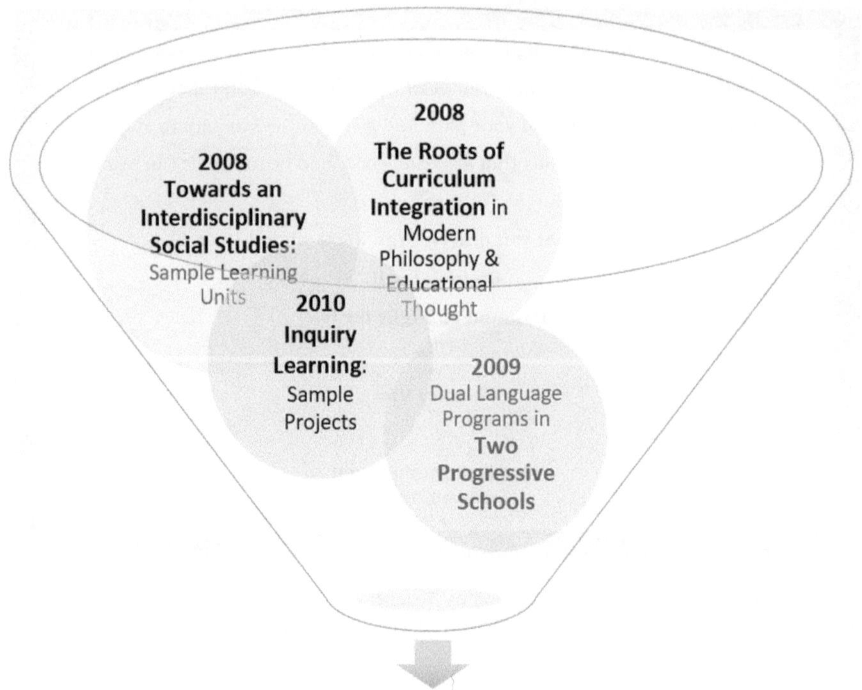

K-12 Teaching Practices

Fig. 1.3 Aleta's conference presentations and publications year 2008–2010. *Note*. Adapted from Villanueva (2019/2021), "Research journey: A tale from the backend". (https://fed.upou.edu.ph/res earch-journeys-2/)

such thing as progressive education in the Philippines; and (2) Teachers were not curricularists, nor curriculum designers.

I thought, precisely the point of my study. I did not say those words as the feeling of disbelief overcame me. Those words hit me hard because first, they negated my lived experiences as a teacher who had worked six years of her early career in a pioneer progressive school in the Philippines. We teachers built the grade-school curriculum from the ground up. Secondly, it was practically saying that the experiences of fellow teacher-leaders and schoolteachers within our network of progressive schools carried no meaning. All throughout, I kept my cool and still tried to respond to their points. But a panel member signaled through a hand gesture which to me corresponded to the command: 'stay!'. It felt like I was a mere university student or a teacher amid education experts or VIPs in my university. In other words, I was just there to take it all in. It felt like a one-way street.

Acting on the suggestion of a faculty member, I took some time to reflect on the experience and I wondered whether there was anything in my proposal which I failed to justify. I was hoping for written feedback or a summary so I could reexamine my

Curriculum Development of Social Studies in Philippine Progressive Schools

by

J. Aleta R. Villanueva

Aim of the Study

The purpose of this study is to:
-narrate the process of curriculum development of the Social Studies in these selected
progressive gradeschools;
-describe the resulting Social Studies curriculum design and elements from these selected
schools;
-discuss the views and conceptions of curriculum designers regarding Social Studies
and curriculum development; and
-examine arising models of curriculum development in the area of Social Studies among
these selected progressive grade schools

Research Questions

As follows are the research questions this study intends to pursue:
1) How is Social Studies curriculum developed, planned and designed in these selected
progressive grade schools?
2) What are the resulting curriculum design and elements of the Social Studies curriculum in
these schools?
3) What are the views and conceptions regarding social studies as a subject matter and its role
in curriculum development in these schools?
4) Are there arising models of curriculum development in the Social Studies among these
selected progressive grade schools?

Methodology

This research intends to operate on these premises:
1) that progressive schools are doing Social Studies differently from mainstream
schools;
2) that progressive school leaders and teachers are viewed as active participants in the
process curriculum development in progressive schools and are therefore considered as
curriculum designers; and,
3) that the researcher, as a teacher herself in a progressive school, is part of the
process of meaning making of the data to be gathered in this research.

Therefore it is through a qualitative methodology this research will take place.

Fig. 1.4 Excerpts from Aleta's 2010 Thesis Topic Proposal. *Note.* A montage of screenshots by
Villanueva (personal communication, May 2, 2010)

work as a way of moving forward. Nothing came. There were no clear procedures nor timelines of what to do next. What was made evident by our graduate school office was that I was close to reaching the maximum residency rule and that I could always request for an extension as did most students. But what I needed was something more. I still wanted to salvage my research topic. I felt that perhaps if gaps or flaws in the different sections in my proposal were pointed out, I could still do better. Or if my adviser could point out weaknesses in my academic writing, then I could spend time to improve it. I would own up to my mistakes and even find ways to work toward the next round of proposal presentations.

After further thought, perhaps I came into my presentation with a clearly biased agenda—to put progressive schools on the map of basic education in the Philippines, and the key role of Social Studies as subject matter which set us apart from other schools. Research to me then was a personal act, an expression of the self and somewhat self-serving. The focus was not solving a problem, nor trying to test a curriculum theory. At this time, I could not ascertain what it meant to have a significant contribution.

After much thought, I decided to give up on that research topic and instead devoted my energies to actual curriculum work at my school. There was so much work to do and projects to enjoy with my school children. I focused on polishing the school's Social Studies program. Eventually, I picked myself up and drew strength improving my craft as a teacher doing classroom-based research. There were other things to be thankful for. I realized for quite some time, I basically operated on the greater need to express my ideas through my first few papers, some of which were published. My writings were a way to gain some form of validation for the work we were doing within my network of schools. They were proof of worthwhile experiments in my K-12 practice which I was able to do on my own terms.

Douglas: From Aleta's reflections and through our joint curation of her experiences, it is evident that developing a research project can be a difficult task. I have experienced this in my own PhD project and in the struggles of many of the research students I have advised over the years. The struggle is caused by different factors, including the need to make an original and significant contribution, issues of scope, personal investment and bias for the topic, meeting discipline requirements, appropriate support and guidance, and identity struggles. To work through these factors, project development can be considered as a process, which moves from initial ideas to an increasingly more concrete and viable project. This can be a messy process which involves planning, engaging with the literature, note taking, discussing ideas with others, and receiving appropriate feedback on writing. One common issue in this process is balancing personal interest and passion for the topic with the requirements and expectations of the discipline.

Like Aleta, I struggled to develop a feasible topic for my PhD. I knew I wanted to investigate something that I was interested in and felt was important. As a longtime practitioner of martial arts, I felt that this was the area I should focus on. I had quite a few ideas for potential research projects in this area that I felt would meet the measure of most research degrees—an original and significant contribution to knowledge. Similar to Aleta's biased agenda to put progressive schools on the map. I had a biased agenda to demonstrate the benefits of martial arts training for cultural and masculine identities. In trying to gain acceptance into a doctoral program, I wrote up many preliminary project proposals and sent them to potential research supervisors all over Australia. I received varying levels of interest in return, but the resounding reply was that the topic was outside of the supervisor's discipline.

At this time, the discipline of Martial Arts Studies was in its very early infancy and was not well established. My suggested topics were too ambitious and required potential supervisors to take a leap of faith into another discipline that did not even exist yet. For beginning research students, understanding the implications of an original and significant contribution is important. Although this refers to breaking exciting new ground, this new ground needs to be connected to existing ways of thinking and discipline specific modalities. My project was seeking to establish the discipline at the same time as my own contribution to knowledge within it. This was too ambitious for one research project. It can be good for research students to have topics they are passionate about and subjectively invested in, but these must also meet the requirements of the discipline and institution. My experiences differed from Aleta's in that I had the support of a colleague to assist me in shaping my project to account for my biased objectives and adjust them to ensure a viable project within the constraints of an established discipline. This ended up being a martial arts based project but framed within the well-defined discipline of sports history.

In my experience this process of project conceptualization and refinement is one most research students struggle with early in their degree. Moving through this process of topic refinement is all part of a developing researcher identity. As our project develops, so do we, as the researcher, develop. We hone the skills of engaging meaningfully with the literature. We begin to understand what it means to think critically as a researcher; and how we might position our project and ourselves within the discipline. This can be a struggle with the self as we transition from a student identity (the project is supported by the identities of others, e.g., the supervisors) to that of researcher (the project is supported by our own sense of self as a researcher). Sometimes it may be a case of straddling both at the same time (Mewburn, 2011) while feeling besieged by imposter syndrome.

At times the struggle may be political and involve more established researchers seeking to privilege their own academic identity over the student researcher (Tyler, 2008). I have seen this type of behaviors on several occasions. One notable example was at a proposal presentation seminar where a senior academic questioned the merits of a student's research project. This is part of the process to ensure a student's project is viable and is usually conducted in a professional and collegial manner. Unfortunately, this was not the case in this situation as the academic continued to ask the same questions repeatedly when it was clear that the student was not yet able to answer them. It was quite uncomfortable as it became clear that this was less about ensuring the project was feasible and more about the academic's own identity and desire to demonstrate his knowledge at the expense of the research student and their project. Bartlett and Eacersall (2019) discuss strategies for individual students to use in these situations, but it would be ideal if they did not occur in the first place.

In Aleta's case she would have benefitted from her institution and the project panel engaging in more supportive rather than gatekeeping-type approaches.

1.1   Research as an Expression of the Self

Some of the issues experienced by Aleta in the shaping of her project were related to her personal investment in the topic (e.g., her life goals and personal educational values) but there were also structural elements (e.g., the approach of the panel, institutional shortcomings and discipline expectations) that added to her negative experience. McAlpine and Amundsen (2018) provide a useful model to understand the interaction of individual and structural elements as part of the research journey (Fig. 1.5). Life goals and values, past experiences, and family relationships are a few examples of personal elements interacting with structural elements, such as institutional approaches in one's identity trajectory and across time.

In Aleta's case, getting into a doctoral program was a convergence of past experiences as a teacher, personal and family relationships, and life goals over and above career goals. However, these came in conflict with structural elements in the form of institutional and discipline expectations of a research degree. This included, justifying to the panel that her project would make an original and significant contribution to the discipline. Aleta's research ideas were natural outcomes of being a teacher in a progressive school environment (Villanueva, 2020), a form of life project and

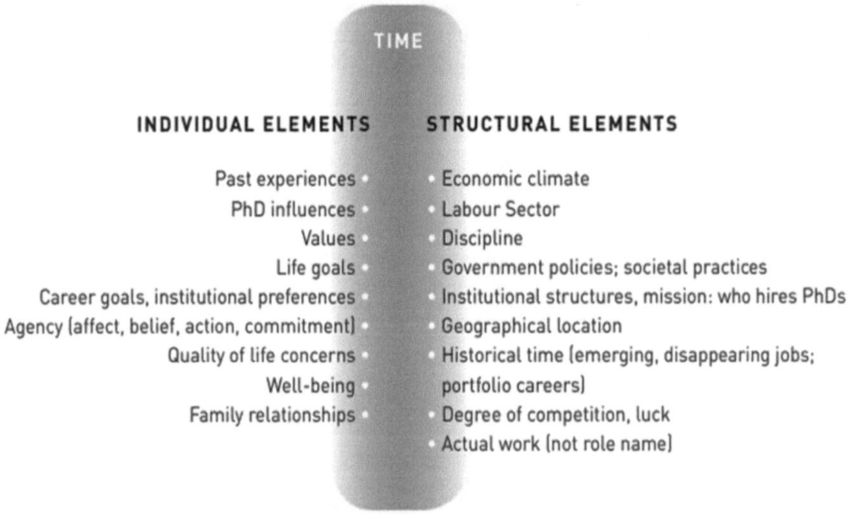

Fig. 1.5 Interaction of individual and structural elements. *Note.* From McAlpine and Amundsen (2018, p. 59), Identity-Trajectories of Early Career Researchers: Unpacking the Post-PhD Experience. Copyright 2018 Palgrave-Macmillan (Springer). Reprinted with permission

early career trajectory, as evidenced by her scholarly writings coming out of her lived experiences of K-12 program development and monitoring. The doctoral study became a means to further her views and personal agenda of progressive education in her home country which filtered into the types of scholarly work she engaged in. This is a concrete example of how an original and significant contribution may be conceptualized based on one's work practice and accompanying life goals and values, and hence can be deeply personal. It can sometimes be a somewhat selfish act in that it serves a rational kind of self-interest according to Rand's (1964) notion of selfishness. Researchers pursue certain agenda or advocacies through research, and therefore can bring in certain subjectivities to their projects. This is evident in Aleta's and Douglas' reflections on their experiences. What is also clear however, in comparing their experiences, is that the pursuit of a personal agenda does not mean that a project is not viable. With the right support and direction, subjective bias can be accounted for and a project developed that results in significant and beneficial contributions to knowledge.

As Aleta's experience demonstrates, research study can be a complex and challenging journey. Significant challenges identified for research students include supervisory issues, financial pressures, a lack of institutional support, inadequate training initiatives, and dehumanizing processes of university bureaucracy (Beasy et al., 2021). Academic writing can also present challenges, especially in terms of negative self-perception and low self-regulation (Calle-Arango & Ávila Reyes, 2022). These can affect the direction of the writing and the resulting project. Like Aleta, research students have expressed a need for support in writing, including effective feedback and more dedicated institutional spaces for writing (Calle-Arango & Ávila Reyes, 2022). Writing groups (Cahusac de Caux et al., 2017) and specialized writing support (Carter et al., 2020; Starfield, 2016) can be useful in guiding the student through these aspects of research study. To assist with these issues, it is important that institutions have the necessary supports for the research journey, including support for writing, data management, project development, information management, proposal assessment panels, effective supervisory teams, and administrative processes.

It is evident that Aleta would have benefitted from some additional support mechanisms during her journey and that institutions can experience some issues providing the necessary support. A doctoral student's research project is examined based on the merits of a written research proposal. Specific standards and criteria, with the panel of experts vetting whether the thesis proposal and the dissertation will potentially lead to a contribution to the field, sets doctoral writing apart from other forms of writing (Molinari, 2021). The expectations placed on doctoral students can be high. There is at times an assumption that those undertaking the highest levels of academic study should already have high levels of prior knowledge and the necessary skills to easily navigate the way through their studies. This is often not the case however, and the pathways through research study can be confusing and difficult to navigate. Possibly, the expectation is higher when it comes to postgraduate students who are in the teaching profession, already having the license to teach, and therefore knowledgeable, resourceful and assumed to be fully equipped with academic writing skills. However, teachers come from varied backgrounds and may be undergoing shifts in their identities from teacher to education researcher, and are therefore still in need of support as doctoral students.

This chapter highlights the context of Aleta's doctoral student experiences which affirm the variability among doctoral student backgrounds (McAlpine & Amundsen, 2018). The variability suggests that certain opportunities and resources must be put in place within the structure of the institution, administratively, to ensure student success through quality doctoral student supervision, research support, and learning community building. Key to each of these issues is institutional research culture. To develop emerging researcher identities, it is important that the institution encourages a culture of value adding and nurturing rather than gate keeping or elitism. This creates an environment in which the identity trajectory of research students (and all researchers) is more positively assured. It also increases the likelihood of a culture which supports research students with mentoring from research supervisors and research training specialists, as well as the necessary administrative structures to ensure that students know what it is they are supposed to be doing and the direction their research topics should be taking.

References

Bartlett, C. L., & Eacersall, D. C. (2019). Confirmation of candidature: An autoethnographic reflection from the dual identities of student and research administrator. In T. M. Machin, M. Clara, & P. A. Danaher (Eds.), *Traversing the doctorate* (pp. 29–56). Palgrave Macmillan. https://doi.org/10.1007/978-3-030-23731-8_3

Beasy, K., Emery, S., & Crawford, J. (2021). Drowning in the shallows: An Australian study of the PhD experience of wellbeing. *Teaching in Higher Education, 26*(4), 602–618. https://doi.org/10.1080/13562517.2019.1669014

Cahusac de Caux, B. K. C. D., Lam, C. K. C., Lau, R., Hoang, C. H., & Pretorius, L. (2017). Reflection for learning in doctoral training: Writing groups, academic writing proficiency and reflective practice. *Reflective Practice, 18*(4), 463–473. https://doi.org/10.1080/14623943.2017.1307725

Calle-Arango, L., & Ávila Reyes, N. (2022). Obstacles, facilitators, and needs in doctoral writing: A systematic review. *Studies in Continuing Education,* 1–19. https://doi.org/10.1080/0158037X.2021.2026315

Carter, S., Guerin, C., & Aitchinson, C. (2020). *Doctoral writing.* Springer.

McAlpine, L., & Amundsen, C. (2018). Identity-trajectories of early career researchers. *Palgrave Macmillan.* https://doi.org/10.1057/978-1-349-95287-8

Mewburn, I. (2011). Troubling talk: Assembling the PhD candidate. *Studies in Continuing Education, 33*(3), 321–331. https://doi.org/10.1080/0158037x.2011.585151

Molinari, J. (2021). Re-imagining doctoral writings as emergent open systems. In C. Badenhorst, B. Amell, J. Burford & K. P. Peirce (Eds.), *Re-imagining doctoral writing* (pp. 49–69). The WAC Clearing House. https://doi.org/10.37514/INT-B.2021.1343.1.3

Rand, A. (1964). *The virtue of selfishness.* Penguin.

Starfield, S. (2016). Supporting doctoral writing at an Australian university. *Writing & Pedagogy, 8*(1). https://doi.org/10.1558/wap.v8i1.27632

The Builders' School, Inc. (2015). The blueprint yearbook sy 2014–2015. *The Builders' School, Building Ideas, Crafting Solutions Incorporated.* https://sites.google.com/view/buildersblueprint2016/t-o-y/school-directors-message-the-blueprint-2014

Tyler, M. A. (2008). The whisperings of a Doctor of Philosophy student's phenomenography. *International Journal of Pedagogies and Learning, 4*(2), 6–14. https://doi.org/10.5172/ijpl.4.1.6

Villanueva, J.A.R. (2010, December 31). The personal is political. *Scratch Paper: Aleta's Evolving Quests, Confusions and Equilibrium.* https://thisisgettingitchy.blogspot.com/2010/

Villanueva, J. A. R. (2019, November 15). *Research journey: A tale from the backend.* [Paper presentation]. 24th Postgraduate and Early Career Research Symposium, University of Southern Queensland, Toowoomba, Australia.

Villanueva, J. A. R. (2020). Transplanting ideas in the Social Studies: Growing inquiry learning. In A. Almario & T. Zamora (Eds.), *School is life: The history of progressive education in the Philippines* (pp. 71–84). Ateneo Press.

Villanueva, J. A. R. (2021, March 18). *PhD v.1.0 ~ v.1.0: A tale from the backend.* [Webinar]. EDUkussion Research Journeys II: The Birthing of Research Ideas and Theses Topics, University of the Philippines Open University Faculty of Education, Philippines. https://fed.upou.edu.ph/research-journeys-2/

Chapter 2
Battlefield 2.0

Abstract In this chapter we outline the prolonged development of a viable student research topic. Our reflections on research student journeys are used to consider the importance of a student's past experiences and interactions in research project refinement. The process of this refinement is outlined, and writing and verbal discussions with significant others are suggested to assist with project conceptualization. Workplace learning and concepts emerging from identity-trajectory theory are discussed as lenses to demonstrate the significance of self in undertaking postgraduate research. In the case of our reflections here, experiences as an academic and work in community-based education directed the student toward a practical roots-based research project, that not only led to a viable research topic but also a sense of remaining true to herself in making an ongoing contribution to teaching and learning in the Philippines' context. The chapter demonstrates that prior to, and also throughout the research journey, the student's experiences and interactions can be integral to the topic and a burgeoning researcher identity.

Keywords Doctoral Education · Research student · Student experience · Student success · Researcher identity · Higher Degree by Research · HDR · Postgraduate Research · PGR · Identity-trajectory

Aleta: Alongside setting up a small progressive school, I also maintained a full-time position as an Assistant Professor at a local open university. This involved additional administrative duties as Program Chair of an undergraduate program. My main task was to provide online academic advice to more than two hundred adult learners seeking to earn a university degree. At the time, I reflected on my workplace experiences as indicated in this excerpt from a paper presented at the Symbiosis International Conference of Open and Distance Learning:

> My initial experiences with fully online learners at an open university generally left me frustrated. This frustration, I recall, was compounded with other factors such as dwelling in my feelings of isolation. There I was in a cubicle thinking through ways to improve my online teaching and almost blaming myself for not challenging the students enough. I often found myself waiting for student responses to my discussion forum and assignment submission bin. Worst, I had no one to talk to, unlike in my former work environments when any co-teacher was within my reach to consult and share stories with.

   15
J. A. R. Villanueva and D. C. F. Eacersall, *Autoethnographic Reflections on a Research Journey*, SpringerBriefs in Education, https://doi.org/10.1007/978-981-99-4929-8_3

It was during my first experience of teaching Philippine History that I got a dose of the range of learners who were part of our undergraduate associate degree program. Mid-semester, when assignments were pouring in, I started reading their life stories as part of their online coursework. I think some of my students had a tough life. I was never placed in a position to choose between studies or supporting a family as a young adult, but my students were taking risks, embracing major responsibilities and making tough choices here and there. (Villanueva, 2011a, pp. 4–5)

In this battle came the need to connect with my students and most of all to connect with fellow faculty members so that I could strategize ways to gain support for my students' needs. I started googling cofaculty members: Who were they? What were their backgrounds and interests? Are they undergoing similar issues? Or am I an isolated misfit? Then I chanced upon the virtual community site of the university:

This virtual site allowed me to see the site members as representatives of the current under-graduate population and the graduate students to some extent. Some have shared pieces of themselves which I think I would not have known on an ordinary day at the Learning Center… I would sometimes have ideas in my brain as I interacted face-to-face with fellow faculty members. Then I'd go to the site to give the students a pinch. I get immediate feedback from students to plan for things which I think they need or will be really good for them. These plans, of course, are materialized after further discussions with faculty members. Now, I'm glad to say that we have additional courses in the program which were a product of interaction with students at the site… The site documented slices of all these initiatives from both students and reliable faculty members who cared to respond... all these to identify with the 'university of the people' (Villanueva, personal communication, June 24, 2010).

* * *

I initially found it peculiar when Prof. Aleta Villanueva, the chair of our associate degree program started using the site as a springboard for academic-related activities. I certainly did not have that level of integration to course work in mind. This led into a blurring of the line between the curricular and the extra-curricular in her program and its students, which currently makes up the majority of active community members. This, so far, is the best example I have seen of the Community Site having a direct hand in improving the learning experience of open university students. – Site Moderator (Villanueva & Librero, 2010, p. 9).

Aleta: The social interactions I engaged in through the open university's virtual community site, collegial communications by email, and face-to-face interactions with students were indicative of my ongoing quest and intent to fulfill my academic role. Engagement in these online and offline experiences as community building, brought me to a safer space to continue with my teaching and learning explorations as I gradually gained confidence in my new work environment. Concrete actions were undertaken in the areas of academic advising, course proposals and learning support initiatives for the undergraduate students. Both students and colleagues provided affirmation of my efforts which enabled me to realize that aspects of my work mattered to others. All these new-found experiences fulfilled my need to connect and make sense of my evolving academic identity in a higher education work environment.

Thus, my experiences as a novice Assistant Professor and Program Chair led me to research quests in the field of distance education. At this time, I was drawing a lot from my informal learning on the job and was also cross-enrolling in a course at the open university to learn more about the qualitative research methodology applied to distance education. An excerpt from my blog demonstrates my reflective process in identifying my ideas about research and the discovery of complementary qualitative research methods that affirmed my approach.

BLOG POST: ONE MISSING PIECE

MONDAY, DECEMBER 28, 2009

My thinking patterns when doing my research in the past was like this: I have data grounded on my everyday practice or experiences. Then I have this need to document it to make it worth sharing to others. Ideas and reflections of the practice go around my head and I feel that perhaps if I write about these, I would feel some kind of release and that hopefully, when I see it written down and read it, it becomes valid. All the more if somebody else reads it or listens to my presentation, then I realize that my experience does make sense. In the process of writing the research, I look for ways and means to elevate the way I [discuss] the data [grounded] on my experiences. Or perhaps look at the data from another point of view where I can remove myself from the experience, analyze the experience, and go back to my practice with a different way of looking at the experience…This process of learning I am going through I liken to be an ongoing conversation in my brain. I know that at some point I will need my [mentor] teacher to enter and perhaps tell me that this is what I've made sense of so far.

Now, all the above fit in perfectly with what I've chanced upon in a book, details of which are as follows:

Book title: Conceptualizing and Proposing Qualitative Research

Author: Thomas H. Schram

Publisher: Pearson Education, NJ Year 2006, page 21

"This chapter invites you to experience the creative discomfort of working from a fuzzy concern toward a researchable aim. It directs attention to what it means to pose a researchable problem and how you meaningfully engage a topic of inquiry" (p. 21).

Therefore, this is about engaging in a sense of a problem then moving towards a refined definition of a problem. Ain't that a good piece to summarize my thoughts today? It is fine to have a missing piece or several missing pieces. It is all part of the process otherwise what will drive me to complete this. (Villanueva, 2009)

Aleta: I was now discovering the following research areas through my own scholarly reading: (1) sense of community (McMillan & Chavis, 1986; Rovai, 2002), (2) online student support and a reflective practice (Boud et al., 1985; Boyd & Failes, 1983), (3) virtual learning community (Brown, 2001; Jones, 1997); (4) teaching presence (Garrison et al., 2001). Critical discourse and reflection were evident through my initial conference presentations which reported on these university work experiences. This process included discovering my colleagues' research leanings and expertise I could rely on, while continuing the path of qualitative research studies. The blog entry below discusses my experiences with Doctor X (pseudonym) and my evolving confidence in undertaking 'my' type of research.

Blog post: Go for Nothingness = Qualitative Research Experience

Saturday, May 28, 2011

Thanks to Doctor X, now I have a more focused project for a faculty research study grant, with real questions which seem to cap what I want to do, but from a perspective of 'teaching presence' as socially constructed.

After my session with Doctor X, I gave my brain time to settle and rest to reflect on my evolving practice of qualitative research. For this study, that was all I needed = a pair of goggles, nothing else and simply dive into the waters --so my senses are free to immerse in the experience of observing and gathering data to arrive at things I am still uncertain of. I have to let the teaching-learning interactions unfold right before my eyes, transcribe and codify all these until I come out of the water, with something new to contribute to research.

You see, my past research topics were 'safe'. I simply had to reinforce what the literature had already said. The data was available in my classrooms and program/school experiments, virtual communities or my current experiences... then I search for the existing theory behind all these. For who am I to propose a theory if there is something else around I can latch onto? There is fun, comfort and safety in that. Or maybe I just needed all these to get over my self-doubt before I started to take risks and assure myself that yes, I am capable of taking myself seriously, just persevere on this path of learning qualitative research--real time. (Villanueva, 2011b)

Douglas: I have experienced the benefits of expertise from others and increasing confidence in my own doctoral studies. I have also observed this in the research endeavors of many students. Considering Aleta's reflections and my own experience of doctoral study, as a student and a research support specialist, there are many activities research students should engage in to find and refine their research topic. These include, scholarly reading, conceptual planning, note taking, discussions with supervisors and significant others, writing, and receiving feedback. Each of these elements work together to inform the other and the project itself. One that I will reflect on here, due to its importance in Aleta's journey, is writing. Aleta experienced developments in her approach to research and her researcher identity, through research writing/presenting, both of which contributed to the refinement of her final thesis topic.

When writing is mentioned, many research students think of writing the thesis. Although this is an important part of the writing process, writing occurs in many forms throughout the research journey. This can include planning documents, conceptualization, emails to supervisors, note taking, statements of original and significant contribution, coursework assignments, blogging, reflective journaling, abstracts, journal articles, conference papers, thesis statements, and thesis drafting. A great deal of this writing will not make it directly into the thesis but instead informs and reforms our thinking and direction of the project. This is conceptual writing which occurs in the planning and drafting phases of the writing. There are many strategies that can be used to assist with this including conceptual mind-mapping software programs. It is important that students have a strategy that transfers the ideas from their mind and into a format where they can more clearly organize and manipulate them to inform the developing thesis. For Aleta, blogging about her research experiences allowed her to reflect on the complex interaction of ideas and start to make sense of them. For myself, it was writing notes on scrap pieces of paper and taking pictures of these for future reference. These ideas were then transferred to word documents and reflected upon for the development of arguments within my writing. Conceptualizing the research topic and associated research arguments is a complex task. Writing is not just the final product but is a vital part of an ongoing reflective process.

Aleta: The transition from my K-12 practice to higher education work happened a few years after my enrollment in my first doctoral study, hence PhD v.1.0. The personal and professional experiences in this transition were highlighted in my scholarly writings from 2009 onward (Fig. 2.1). These written works served as opportunities for sensemaking and reflection on my teaching and professional practices in a tertiary-level work environment. As such, my conference paper presentations served as opportunities to reflect on my burgeoning research interest in the field of Open and Distance eLearning (ODeL) while also reflecting on my emerging practices in higher education. For example, in my 2011 authored conference paper, I drew from the work of Coats (2005) who indicated that reflective practice works on the assumption that people are predisposed to self-criticism in viewing their work performance.

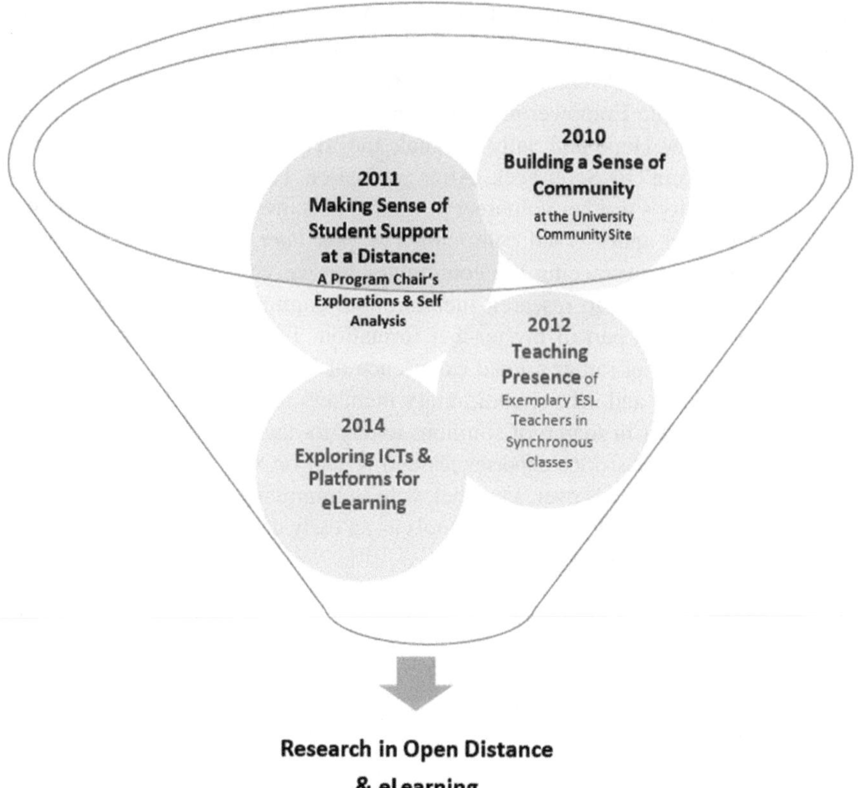

Fig. 2.1 Aleta's scholarly works year 2009 onward. *Note.* Adapted from Villanueva (2019), Research Journeys: A Tale from the Backend

Practitioners go through a process of identifying areas which worked well and areas for improvement. "Reflection that leads to improvement involves a willingness to learn and change" (Coats, 2005, p. 3). The reflection undertaken was on my multiple roles, that is as a Program Chair providing academic advice and student support, as an Assistant Professor handling teacher education courses and this time as a higher education researcher.

My willingness to learn filtered through the widening of research topics and interests. During this period my scholarly work shifted gears which in turn influenced the direction of my proposed doctoral research. Throughout this period of informal workplace learning, reflection and opening up to other possibilities for my research, I discussed, with colleagues in my university of employment, my best friend, and other teacher friends, a potential doctoral research topic in virtual learning communities and eLearning rooted in community building.

Looking back, from 1996 to 1998, I undertook my Masters in Community Development while immersed in community-based education work with a resettled indigenous community in a rural area of the Philippines. This was my first stint of utilizing community building strategies while also running literacy programs with parents and children. Instead of a thesis-track under my MA program, I did field practice to gain more hands-on experience in community work. Through my graduate school readings, I engaged in "Pedagogy of the Oppressed" by Paolo Freire, "Community Organizing for People Empowerment" by Angelito Manalili, "Training for Transformation" by Anne Hope and Sally Timmel, and "The Road Less Travelled" and "The Different Drum" by Scott Peck. After graduation, I became a full-time volunteer in the university's teacher volunteer program. This involved serving as a public schoolteacher in an underserved community. A year later, I became a University Extension Specialist overseeing the community service volunteer program of the university. The exposure to research literature and community immersion experiences were very much part of my teacher formation. Teaching was not just about 'teaching a subject' but rather a lived experience of building rapport and connectedness with students and school community members in remote environments. In other words, a teacher in search of solutions to day-to-day problems in classes will look back to prior classroom experiences and reflect on ways to test or improve pedagogy and practice. However, a teacher, with a community-building thinking hat, coupled with new-found doctoral study tools as an early career researcher, will turn to research to solve problems in education.

Douglas: Much can be learnt from Aleta's experiences of a developing research topic and associated academic/researcher identity. The research topic is often influenced by significant others and the activities the researcher engaged/engages in. A vital element in the process of developing ideas and arguments is discussion of thoughts with relevant others. The most useful discussions will usually be undertaken between a student and their supervisors, but this is not always the case. Like Aleta, it might also involve conversations with colleagues and/or significant others, such as friends or family members. What is important is that the student has someone they can talk to and voice their thoughts with. This allows the thoughts to take shape and develop as they are voiced aloud. Supervisors and colleagues are most useful as they can usually add to the discussion and point the researcher in productive directions. I remember discussions with academics, who were not my supervisors, at pivotal stages of my PhD project. I will forever be grateful to these individuals for guiding these discussions in ways that developed me as a researcher and my project in positive directions. I am also grateful to my family members, who would patiently 'listen' as I talked through my developing research project. The ability to voice my ideas to someone was always useful as verbalization helped to organize and shape them. All these elements, engaging with the literature, writing, and scholarly interactions with our professional and personal networks, are part of the research process. They are also forms of reflective practice. These, along with our past experiences and sense of who we are, feed into the progressive development of the project and the development of the self as scholarly researcher.

2.1 Research as a Reflective Practice

Research this time around was a form of reflective practice for Aleta, likewise a sensemaking and scholarly identity building process as she confronted new-found experiences of being a doctoral student and faculty member engaged in an open university. The process of reflective learning, within reflective practice, is highlighted by Boyd and Failes (1983) as follows:

- A sense of inner discomfort
- Identification or clarification of the concern
- Openness to new information from internal and external sources, with ability to observe and take in from a variety of perspectives
- Resolution, expressed as 'integration', 'coming together', 'acceptance of self-reality', and 'creative synthesis'
- Establishing continuity of self with past, present, and future
- Deciding whether to act on the outcome of the reflective process (p. 106)

To address inner discomfort in workplace adjustment, Aleta turned to research literature for answers. This was partly borne out of doctoral experience wherein valuable book references and journal articles sparked curiosity and served as sources of knowledge. The revival of research interest in 'community development' turned into concrete knowledge products in the form of Aleta's initial published works, a form of coming together or creative synthesis for that matter. The literature she discovered because of her K-12 community work, found new meaning within the context of her university employment. This is indicative of establishing continuity of the self with the past and present (Boyd & Failes, 1983).

Similarly, doctoral students can take time to reflect on their work scenarios as possible sources of their learning and development as researchers. Confronting the inner discomfort fuels one to move forward and explore possibilities in one's research project and even if it entails stepping out of one's comfort zone to delve into other research topics. Moving forward also means acknowledging one's prior mistakes and limitations. Instead of viewing these as barriers they can be used as opportunities to take risks and find new directions in one's research interests. In Aleta's case, her sustained interest to learn and theorize, from her work experiences and advocacies, allowed her to learn from the research literature, and those in her network, and persist in her doctoral journey.

Scholarly identity is reported to be constructed over time as doctoral students pursue thinking and their learning intent through seeking validation from their intellectual and institutional networks (McAlpine & Amundsen, 2018). The quality of opportunities to exercise independent voice, and the nature of support experienced from one's network, affect one's experience of scholarly identity (Cotterall, 2015). Aleta's source of validation included real-life experience of virtual community building with students and colleagues, who occupied her personal and professional circles. Likewise, this is a clear example of drawing from personal and institutional networks to build a scholarly identity. The reflection and action was undertaken rather informally and voluntarily, outside Aleta's expected duties of teaching and administrative work. This resulted in a widening of research interests outside the comfort zone of K-12 classroom teaching practices and curriculum studies of doctoral coursework to reveal an evolving scholarly identity moving toward open and distance eLearning.

Research as a reflective practice in Aleta's narrative likewise highlights the intellectual strand of identity-trajectory as influenced by past engagements. This connection which depicted the beginnings of her scholarly identity was not explicitly apparent to her in 2009, but rather intuitively as she blogged about her research process. Although Aleta's work experience did not directly result in her earning her doctoral degree, it did enrich her experiences which became sources of learning, reflection and writings, a seedbed for prospective research ideas. This experience was indicative of workplace learning, a well-researched area in teacher professional learning and identity development. Workplace learning involves learning from experience "embedded in everyday practices, action and conversation" (Fenwick, 2008, p. 19). School teachers (K-12) have used this approach in their higher education research to examine their identity development (Russo, 2020; van Lankveld et al., 2017) and so, this is a fitting lens to examine identity development within doctoral student experiences and in particular that of teacher-researchers or teacher professionals moving into university work, hence the shift or widening of possible research areas from the K-12 and higher education or in Aleta's case that of a face-to-face teaching practice to that of an online learning environment.

Likewise, it is also fitting that the discussion that follows superimposes the identity-trajectory in order to appreciate past events in the context of one's construction of the present. Tracing the beginnings of Aleta's scholarly pursuits is best understood using the idea of the identity-trajectory which considers the influence of past events on one's intentions for undergoing a doctoral study (McAlpine & Amundsen, 2018). In reflecting on Aleta's experiences, this can be extended to also include the influence of past events and experiences on not only coming to the research topic but also its ongoing development. In this way researchers bring themselves, including their ideas, experiences, and skills as tools to be used on the whole research journey.

Their sense of self shapes the research project and as they progress, their experiences in developing the research project begin to shape their identities and skills as researchers and academics. According to the tenets of identity-trajectory, learning is viewed as developmental and lifelong. This view engages an interpretation of one's life choices and intentions and relates these to one's present and future BE-comings. This kind of sensemaking is integral to Aleta's professional and scholarly experiences. The action-reflection as embedded in her scholarly writings likewise indicate a sense of agency—not dictated by the institution nor her actual doctoral coursework requirements, but rather rooted on her scholarly identity construction throughout time. The scholarly identity is still an extension of her teacher identity as molded in part by past experiences of community-based teaching and initial graduate level work. All of Aleta's scholarly endeavors led to her eventual PhD v.2.0 topic which is discussed fully in Part 2 of this book. This took some time to eventuate and involved the demise of Aleta's PhD v.1.0 as narrated in the next chapter.

References

Boud, D., Keogh, R., & Walker, D. (1985) *Reflection: Turning experience into learning*. Kegan Page.

Boyd, E. M., & Failes, A. L. (1983). Reflective learning: Key to learning from experience. *Journal of Humanistic Psychology, 23*(2), 99–117. https://doi.org/10.1177/002216788323232011

Brown, R. E. (2001). The process of community-building in distance learning classes. *Journal of Asynchronous Learning Networks, 5(2)*, 18–35. https://doi.org/10.24059/olj.v5i2.1876

Coats, M. (2005, September 20–23). *Reflection revisited: Can it really enhance practice?* 11th Cambridge International Conference on Open and Distance Learning. The Open University Centre for Outcomes-Based Education. Cambridge, UK.

Cotterall, S. (2015). The rich get richer: International doctoral candidates and scholarly identity. *Innovations in Education and Teaching International, 52*(4), 360–370.

Fenwick, T. (2008). Workplace learning: Emerging trends and new perspectives. *New Directions for Adult and Continuing Education, 2008*, 17–26. https://doi.org/10.1002/ace.302

Garrison, D. R., Anderson, T., & Archer, W. (2001). Critical thinking, cognitive presence, and computer conferencing in distance education. *American Journal of Distance Education, 15*(1), 7–22. https://doi.org/10.1080/08923640109527071

Jones, Q. (1997). Virtual-communities, virtual settlements & cyber-archaeology: A theoretical outline. *Journal of Computer-Mediated Communication, 3*(3), Article No. 2. https://doi.org/10.1111/j.1083-6101.1997.tb00075.x

McAlpine, L., & Amundsen, C. (2018). Identity-trajectories of early career researchers: Unpacking the post-PhD experience. *Palgrave Macmillan.* https://doi.org/10.1057/978-1-349-95287-8

McMillan, D. W., & Chavis, D. M. (1986). Sense of community: A definition and theory. *Journal of Community Psychology, 14*(1), 6–22. https://doi.org/10.1002/1520-6629(198601)14:1%3C6::aid-jcop2290140103%3E2.0.co;2-i

Rovai, A. P. (2002). Building sense of community at a distance. *The International Review of Research in Open and Distributed Learning, 3*(1), 1–16. https://doi.org/10.19173/irrodl.v3i1.79

Russo, J. A. (2020). The experiences and identity structures of teacher-researcher hybrid professionals in a primary school mathematics context. *EURASIA Journal of Mathematics, Science and Technology Education, 16*(7). https://doi.org/10.29333/ejmste/8250

Schram, T. H. (2006). *Conceptualizing and proposing qualitative research*. Pearson/Merrill Prentice-Hall.

Van Lankveld, T., Schoonenboom, J., Volman, M., Croiset, G., & Beishuizen, J. (2017). Developing a teacher identity in the university context: A systematic review of the literature. *Higher Education Research & Development, 36*(2), 325–342. https://doi.org/10.1080/07294360.2016.1208154

Villanueva, J.A.R. (2009, December 28). The missing piece. *Scratch Paper: Scratch Paper: Aleta's Evolving Quests, Confusions and Equilibrium.* https://thisisgettingitchy.blogspot.com/2009/12/missing-piece.html

Villanueva, J.A.R., & Librero, A.F.D. (2010, June 29–July 1). Building a sense of community at the UP Open University community site. [Paper Presentation]. ICT, 2010 Villanueva, J.A.R., & Librero, A.F.D. (2010, June 29-July 1).*Building a sense of community at the UP Open University community site.* [Paper Presentation]. ICT 2010 Singapore Conference. SIM University, Singapore.

Villanueva, J. A. R. (2011a, February 21–23). *Making sense of student support at a distance: A program chair's explorations and self-analysis.* [Paper presentation] Symbiosis International Conference of Open and Distance Learning, Pune, India.

Villanueva, J.A.R. (2011b, May 28). Go for nothingness=QualiR experience. *Scratch Paper: Aleta's Evolving Quests, Confusions and Equilibrium.* https://thisisgettingitchy.blogspot.com/2011/05/skinnydippingnothingness-qr-experience.html

Villanueva, J.A.R. (2019, November 15). *Research journey: A tale from the backend.* [Paper presentation]. 24th Postgraduate and Early Career Research Symposium, University of Southern Queensland, Toowoomba, Australia.

Chapter 3
The Bitter and the Sweet

Abstract The student research journey can be a bumpy road with many ups and downs. In this chapter we reflect on the positive and negative experiences of the student journey with a focus on enablers that can support and motivate students to persevere. Through our reflections we demonstrate how the accumulation of institutional barriers, research difficulties, and the challenges of everyday life can have a liminal and emotional effect, placing students' mental health and wellbeing at risk. The ability and motivation to continue study in these cases often depend on each student's particular circumstances. In the case of the research student examined in this chapter, feelings of national and social responsibility were important factors in her decision to persevere. Significant others including work colleagues, friends, and family also played a vital role. We conclude that more recognition, research, and institutional support needs to be invested to address the difficulties research students can experience. This approach should include elements to ensure adequate and appropriate support from the supervisory team and must also consider the effective integration of additional support networks such as colleagues, research groups, friends, family, and university support services. The significance of this approach is that it provides a supportive research culture for students when things are going poorly that does not rely only on the supervisory team. These types of approaches can also benefit all students to ensure the best experience and student success during both the ups and the downs of the research journey.

Keywords Doctoral Education · Research student · Student experience · Student success · Wellbeing · Researcher identity · Higher Degree by Research · HDR · Postgraduate Research · PGR · Liminality · Affect · Rite of passage

© The Author(s), under exclusive license to Springer Nature Singapore Pte Ltd. 2023
J. A. R. Villanueva and D. C. F. Eacersall, *Autoethnographic Reflections on a Research Journey*, SpringerBriefs in Education, https://doi.org/10.1007/978-981-99-4929-8_4

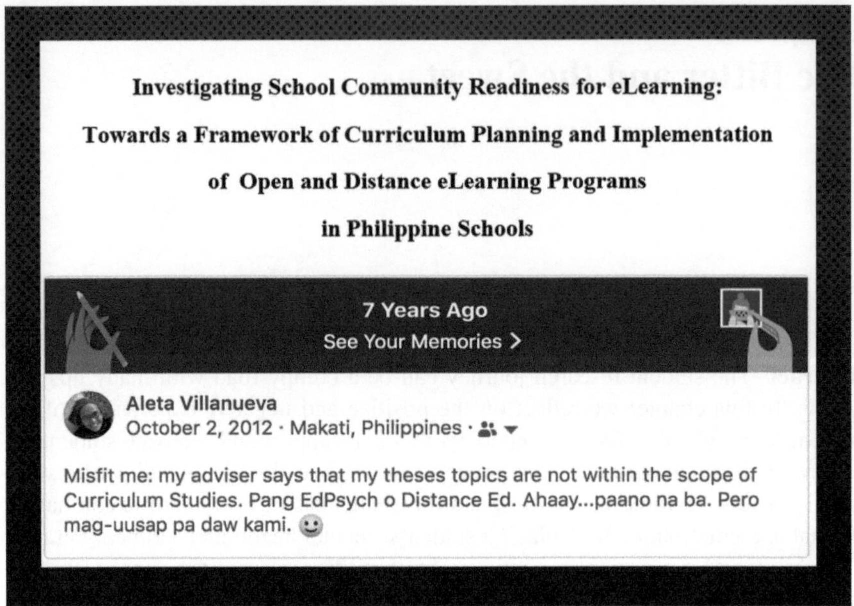

Fig. 3.1 A montage of Aleta's research proposal and Facebook post. *Note.* Image adapted from
a slide presentation by Villanueva (2019, November) and with translation: "it is in the area of
Educational Psychology or Distance Education. Oh my, how is this now? But then, we will continue
to talk about it"

> This gets in conflict with external pressure to acquire a PhD because this is what is acceptable
> to the academic world. A PhD is a necessity in a higher ed career. Academics and scholars are
> supposed to generate knowledge. This I question of course. There's just too much knowledge
> to go around with, right? The greater need for me, is to write what I want to write.
>
> So it's still an ongoing battle of wills: a part of me says "Wisen up!", a part of me says "Give
> it up!" and yet one says, "Give it a rest...let things be". (Villanueva, 2010b)

Aleta: By 2012, having hurdled a few workplace adjustments in my university and
gaining confidence as a university-based teacher educator, I dared to once again,
engage in a research topic proposal presentation. My adviser was trying to redirect
me to do a curriculum evaluation of the open high school system. But being an
outsider to the open high school, I felt that the task of evaluation coming from a
research student was not timely nor proper given that the open high school was still
carving its place in the K-12 setting. Instead, I was interested in school community
readiness for eLearning as depicted in Fig. 3.1.

At my proposal presentation, the panel members said that my scope was no longer
within the area of Curriculum Studies as my topic was framed from the perspective
of Distance Education. This meant that once again my aspirations to proceed with the
needed research proposal approval did not materialize. After this round of rejection
of my second research proposal, I felt tired and exhausted. I was getting frustrated

with myself for 'missing the mark' and having research topics which did not seem to fit the mold.

Looking back, the feeling of rejection from my panel unearthed memories and feelings of being alienated at certain points of my life because either I felt different, or my ideas and perspectives were not the same as others. As the lone Protestant student, who did not join confessions nor rosary prayers, at an all-girls private Catholic school I had always felt like the odd one out. At one point, I wanted to change my name in order to conform since I did not have a Mary, an angel nor a saint's name anywhere in my full name.

Eventually I embraced 'being different' as I entered a non-sectarian university where diversity of ideas, backgrounds and talents were accepted as part of life. I thought I was over those moments of alienation only to encounter it once again. Thus, the terrible feeling during my second panel presentation seemed familiar. For the first time, I questioned my intellectual and emotional ability to cope with my studies and my issues. It did not help that I was also going through a midlife crisis and questioning my life choices regarding marriage and motherhood.

The self-doubt sank in deeper when my husband and I read through my son's neuropsychological report. We both suspected a form of learning disability, a condition he was able to cope with for the first few years of his school life as he had made steady gains in his reading. By Grade 3 however, the signs were manifesting in his written work. Reading the descriptions of my son's learning difficulties in the areas of written expression, executive functions, and working memory felt like a description of my own learning issues. Seeing, in print, the difficulties my son was going through enabled me to acknowledge some of these repressed feelings and self-perceived limitations. It motivated me to end my misery and find a better environment to help me through my studies.

BLOG POST: THESIS…ANTI-THESIS, AND SO I GO ON THIS WAY

FRIDAY, DECEMBER 21, 2012

These 2 weeks I badly need to reformulate my topic proposal. I am now back to rethinking about my original topic. Now if only I can get rid of these: anger towards a faculty member who did not respond to my first few emails about my topic…anger at myself for having such a muddled brain which can never work for a sustained, and focused study on this thing called thesis.

Thesis work entails a disciplined mind which practically goes against the fiber of how my brain is wired. But because I still believe in the power of the mind and rational thinking, it goes to show that I just need to rewire ME. (Villanueva, 2012)

3.1 Barriers Moving Forward

Aleta: This brings me to reflect on the personal barriers of my PhD v.1.0 journey, one of which was going through a depressive cycle, and perhaps a midlife crisis. I met with three counselors during these times spanning my PhD v.1.0. While I have yet to discern whether my depression was rooted in my higher education studies, what I can say is this: my work and my research writing was a way to keep my rational mind going, while all else seemed to fall apart.

Some barriers were clearly institutional, for example, the lack of checks and balances in research supervision and professional communication of the research process. Another barrier was the lack of mentoring and supervising techniques to accommodate learners, such as I, whose brains are wired differently. The only way out of a research adviser-advisee relationship mismatch for me was to sever ties. Although I was Assistant Professor in another autonomous campus under the same university system, it was clear to me that I was a mere student, and the expectation was that I would be the only one doing any necessary adjustments.

Other barriers came in the form of specific criteria for admission into programs which I was not able to satisfy, in my home country and other universities in Asia. These seem to be institutional limitations in terms of fewer doctoral offerings, and a lack of flexibility and recognition of prior knowledge and work experience. For example, I was interested in doing a doctoral program with a specialization in Distance Education, but one university only offered Science Education as an area of concentration. I inquired with another open university in Asia having a doctoral program with Distance Education as its specialization, but this could only be under-taken through a mix of face-to-face and traditional mail-based distance education modes. It was not a fully online program allowing me to stay in the Philippines with my family and maintain my usual work. Another open university in Southeast Asia had a list of coursework I found most ideal given its online courses. However, it required a master's degree in education as an entry requirement. Despite my years of work experience in education, I still did not qualify since my education degree was at the bachelor's level.

With much thought, I was accountable for my self-doubt and indecisiveness resulting from a desperate need to nail a research proposal worthy of approval. I was questioning if I was getting into a PhD for the right reasons and whether employ-ment in higher education was for me. I was also starting to question the idea of a PhD itself and its value in my academic work. With one year remaining before reaching an extended maximum doctoral residency, I was determined to exit as I felt that I could not continue to stretch my mental capabilities.

Douglas: The research student journey can be like a roller coaster with many ups and downs along the track. Research students have particular learning needs that require specialized assistance and support (Eacersall, 2018). As a learning advisor and researcher development specialist for research student programs, I have often assisted students during difficult times. Project conceptualization, juggling family responsibilities, access to participants or equipment, supervisory problems, illness, stress, anxiety, writing the thesis and more recently COVID-19 are some of the common issues I have helped students with. I remember as a young child riding the ghost train with my mother at the local show. The ups and downs were scary, as were props along the way but there was one part of the ride that really made me jump. It was near the end just after the final bend—a mirrored saloon style set of doors that allowed an up-close glimpse of my own reflection before we hurtled through it and the ride was over. Just like that mirror, and other challenging life experiences, the student research journey can shine a light on ourselves accentuating our strengths and weaknesses, amplifying issues such as self-doubt, research fatigue and imposter syndrome. At times the reflection can become so intense that a pressure cooker of anxiety and depression forms. Studies into research student wellbeing demonstrate just how serious this situation can be (Beasy et al., 2021; Brownlow et al., 2022; Guthrie et al., 2017). I know during my own journey there were times that I felt confused, or trapped, like I could not breathe. These were times that as I reflected on my project, I could not see the way forward. It seemed no matter how hard I worked there were no solutions, no way out and no way to progress. I remember walking around the gardens at my university in tears because it all seemed so hopeless. Research can be challenging and at these times it is especially important that students can access support and guidance to help them find their way.

Research support professionals and supervisors play an important role in guiding students to negotiate the ups and downs of the research journey. Through reflection on my own professional practice, I have identified a five-step approach to provide students with emotional support and practical options. (1) Listen actively. The significance of this point cannot be overemphasized. Active listening with questions and prompts interspersed along the way ensures that the supervisor or support staff fully understand the perspective of the student and the issues they are experiencing. (2) Demonstrate genuine empathy. It is important the student feels that you understand their circumstances and that you care for their wellbeing. The further away one's own research student journey becomes the easier it can be to forget how difficult the journey was. For some supervisors the emphasis can be getting more students through in less time rather than nurturing students through the difficult periods. Within the current neoliberal university setting, focused on completions, completion times, and number of publications, it is even more vital that students feel they are getting empathetic support from supervisors and significant others. (3) Provide options rather than solutions. It is important that the student fully understands the options available to them so that they can make their own informed decisions to move forward. This assists students in gaining a sense of control over situations that may feel out of control. (4) Assist the student to develop a plan. It is important that the student makes a plan and that the feasibility of the plan is discussed. This gives them something concrete and achievable to work toward. (5). Refer to professional counseling services. Sometimes it is appropriate to refer the student to professional counseling services. These professionals can provide students with strategies and treatment plans to help with the issues students may be dealing with.

Many students will negotiate their way through troubling times and continue with their studies. Others, as was the case with Aleta, may withdraw from the program. Withdrawal should not be viewed as failure. Once all the different options have been considered, it can be the best decision. What is of paramount importance is that the student can choose the best option for themselves given their circumstances. I have helped many students with this decision who, after withdrawing from the program, have returned to successfully finish their research degree at a more suitable time.

Often, as was the case with Aleta, the time and circumstances of research degree 1.0 or even 2.0 are not right. It is much better to take some time out and come back to it when the likelihood of a happier journey is more assured.

3.2 The Sweet

Aleta: A few months after exiting my doctoral program, I started anew with university applications. This time I dared to go for universities in Australia. One university required a higher IELTS score and academic references. Another found my qualification acceptable but could not find a supervisor to match my research agenda. Feedback on my applications assured me that my emerging thesis was worth looking into. My thesis was taking shape as I composed different versions of preliminary research proposals to go with my university applications. For a Doctor of Education program I was applying for, I included the following in my email correspondence:

TIMESTAMP: JUNE 4, 2013, 11:51 AM

Specifically, I intend to investigate the educational experiences of Filipino teachers and learners in a blended course of the Philippine Open High School system (OHSS) through the lens of teaching presence (TP) and learning presence (LP). TP is an element from the Communities of Inquiry framework (COI) (Anderson et al., 2001), while LP is a recently proposed element (Shea et al., 2012), both of which are constructs studied in higher education online learning environments, but have yet to be applied in the context of secondary level teaching and learning. Through this initial investigation, a blended course shall be designed and implemented in order to reexamine the interaction of TP and LP, and the resulting educational experiences of teachers and learners. The study seeks to contribute a new way of looking at the COI framework and its elements and how this can be utilized in virtual/ open schooling systems. (Villanueva, personal communication, June 4, 2013)

The basic education in the Philippines has shifted from a ten-year education program to a twelve-year program. With this shift, there were adjustments for the general education curriculum at the tertiary level. My curiosity regarding virtual high schools started in 2011, and by 2014, while on a two-year leave from my academic position, I was fortunate to be situated in my daughter's high school which allowed me to see other possibilities for my thesis. I was learning the ins and outs of a high school, and more importantly the curriculum of Grades 9–12 based on internationally accredited standards. I engaged with a little literature in my country's open high school system and other alternative learning programs. My other ideas were to bridge the general education of senior high school (Year 11 and 12) to university level work through open and distance learning. I was also considering possible links in the areas of open resource development and teacher education through service and extension work (Fig. 3.1). I went as far as imagining and conceptualizing a progressive school version of an open high school becoming a lab school for our open university student-teachers, education studies, and multimedia undergraduates (Villanueva, 2014b).

I managed to safekeep all these ideas as I crafted different versions of my rejected research proposals on eLearning and virtual and open high schools. It was genuine feedback from two Australian universities which assured me that there was something to my research interests and that perhaps it was a matter of finding the right match—a mentor, a program, and a university where my research ideas could fit in.

3.3 Motivations

Aleta: Throughout the challenges at different points of my PhD v.1.0 from 2004 to 2012, I managed to persevere. In the most testing of times, I would always look back to why I decided to become a teacher and remain in the Philippines. I had imbibed the university's mission early on when I was once part of its extension program as a pioneer teacher volunteer to the barrios. The goal of the volunteer corps was "to make the University a more caring academic community that is bound together by a commitment to the empowerment of the people and selfless service to the nation…" (Ugnayan ng Pahinungod, 2000, backcover). I share these ideals with my husband and teacher-friends who are fellow graduates of a university, "for the nation, for the people" (Encarnacion, 2017). Giving back to the Filipino people has been impressed upon us by the university encouraging us to be scholars of the nation whose education has been supported by taxpayers from the Filipino masses. With this noble vision are actions and words of inspiration and encouragement from significant others, mainly friends, and colleagues from my open university as seen in the blog excerpt that follows and the digital artifacts depicted thereafter (Figs. 3.2 and 3.3):

BLOG POST: FROM A DEAR COLLEAGUE =)

DECEMBER 1, 2010

On a personal note, I feel that you need to take a breather from your PhD. You've been reading and reading and writing and writing for the past five years…you might need to let the waters sit still so that the muck will go down and the clear water will remain. First let the waters still, then wait for it to clear, and then take a good look at yourself in it. :) It'll be right on target by that time. (Villanueva, 2010a)

Through informal ways and spaces for communicating, meaningful exchanges happened on a variety of concerns and issues which resulted in further reflection and resolution. For example, a sense of significance for our work in our open university, it being an autonomous unit of the system-wide university, was put into words by a senior colleague who was a former Chancellor (Fig. 3.2). During times when we could meet face-to-face, as most of our transactions were held virtually, we talked about our teaching concerns which most often gave way to conversations on our research ideas. In my recollection, in the early days of my growing interest in K-12 virtual schools and Open High School programs, a good colleague-friend spent some time actively listening to my racing thoughts. She calmly jotted down my ideas and questions (Fig. 3.3). All these served as good reminders to press on with ideas

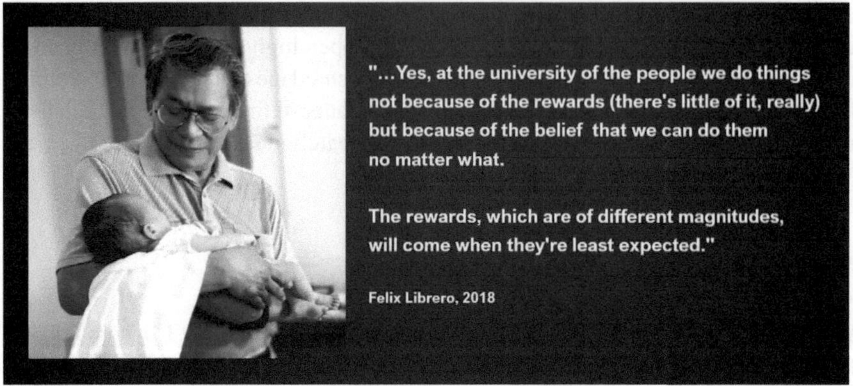

Fig. 3.2 A screenshot of wise words from a colleague. *Note*. Adapted from Villanueva, 2021, "PhD v.1.0 ~ PhD v.2.0: A tale from the backend" (https://fed.upou.edu.ph/research-journeys-2/)

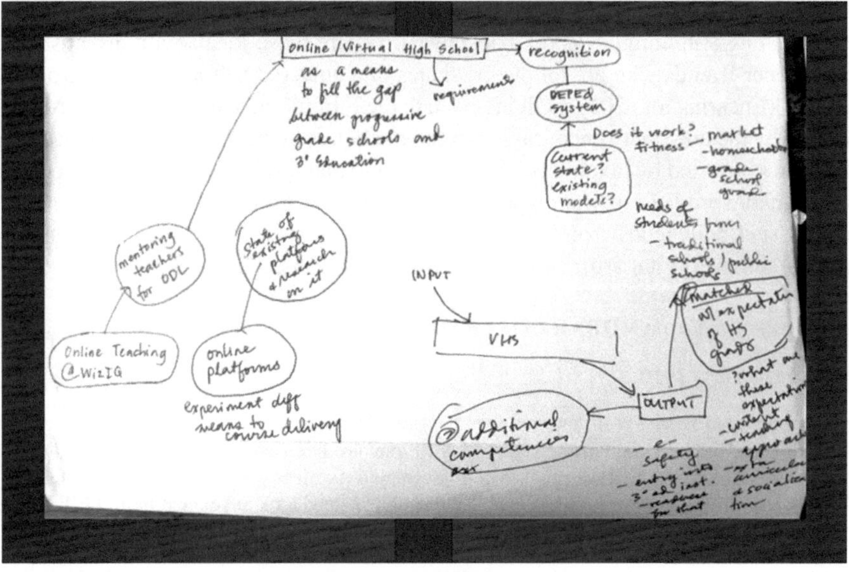

Fig. 3.3 A colleague's mind map of Aleta's evolving research ideas

or plans on program development and administration, public service initiatives and most of all, research.

As members of an academic community, we continued to grow our research ideas bound by a bigger vision and a collective identity of being in a public service university. Hence, the open university was not only a place of work and lifelong learning, but also a community where I felt I belonged. In fact, my colleagues inspired me to do better, and this served as a motivation to press on.

BLOG POST: THESES 2-2B, DRAGONFLY MODE

APRIL 10, 2014

Honestly, and funny as it may seem, I am mostly in awe of my colleagues and how intricate
their perspectives can be whenever we discuss matters of importance, and how I also manage
to put my 2 cents in, because I clearly operate on instinct or use my practical brains mostly
and even if sometimes I simply give up on the process of engaging since somebody more
brilliant will most likely come around to solving matters anyways. Yet, bringing my 2 cents
in comes with the job so I take pains to understand as much as I can how people at my
university arrive at certain decisions. I want to continue being part of this decision making,
life complicating process. And so, I believe, my doctoral degree experience is a chance of
a lifetime to do just that-- prune my brains and discipline my mind (which behaves like a
dragonfly mostly), in order to put my 100 cents in for all that we need to do and accomplish
as a university... I have so much respect for my open university community-- that I can
practically imagine myself growing old in this institution. I have so much respect for it that
if ever I decide to choose to stay, it is because I have earned my keep as much as others ahead
of me already did. Earning my keep, to my mind, is fulfilling this responsibility to get that
PhD-- the right to get into more research to gain proof that I do possess this habit of mind
to think theoretically & reflectively to solve life's problems, to be part of a community of
scholars committed to the excellent pursuit of knowledge! (Villanueva, 2014a)

Another motivation for me to press on was the challenging experience of listening
to student concerns regarding their thesis work. By year 2012, I was already a tenured
faculty member at my university with responsibilities to monitor graduate students.
These were all practicing schoolteachers in the process of undertaking their thesis. I
facilitated communications between prospective research advisers and thesis students
as part of their research topic presentations. My duties were largely administrative
but in the process of listening to their concerns and difficulties, I realized that perhaps
the best way to help these students was to continue undergoing the research journey
myself and, as a student, develop the much-needed skills in research advising and
supervision.

3.4   Research as an Emotional Rite of Passage

The concepts of liminality, rite of passage, and threshold crossing have been discussed
in doctoral research studies to make sense of doctoral experiences (Wisker et al.,
2010). Liminality connotes a state of being in between (Turner, 1977), and as applied
to the doctoral study it is "where one is no longer who previously existed, nor has
yet developed into the independent researcher or expert practitioner" (Keefer, 2015,
p.18). Not much is known about how doctoral students experience this (Buirski,
2021), though Keefer (2015) described the doctoral liminal phase as a highly personal
experience characterized by confusion, uncertainty, and lack of confidence. This is
similar to Aleta's experience at certain points in her research journey, for example
transitioning from doctoral coursework to the thesis proposal phase. This was a rite
of passage of an emotional kind, the examination of which highlights the importance
of threshold and liminal concepts and their application in the context of student

research study; liminality, significant events and affect; personal agency and affect; and, becoming and significant others in the student research journey.

3.4.1 Threshold and Liminal Concepts and Their Application

The concepts of thresholds and liminality in research student training are useful as they consider learning as a transformative process of overcoming difficult sticking points during the student journey. In this way, threshold concepts represent "a transformed way of understanding, or interpreting, or viewing something without which the learner cannot progress" (Meyer & Land, 2006, p. 3). Just how long the learner may be stuck on the threshold, unable to progress, can be momentary or more prolonged and 'troublesome' (Meyer & Land, 2006). This period of passing through the threshold has been termed a liminal state (Kiley, 2009). This is a state of being in between or transitioning from one state to another. It represents the state in which a student is on the cusp of reaching an understanding or milestone but has not quite passed through to the other side yet. An analogy of the Buddhist temple threshold is helpful to understand these concepts and how they affect a student's journey and learning experience.

Buddhist temples often have quite a high threshold at their entrance. This can sometimes be as high as 30 cm. When crossing this threshold, it is considered impolite to step on the threshold itself, and so one must step over the threshold, one foot at a time. This means that there is a period in which one is straddling the threshold with one foot on either side. This is a liminal state in which the temple goer is both inside the temple and outside, and yet at the same time is neither fully inside the temple nor fully outside. They are in a state of in between. Some thresholds can also be quite broad stretching the visitor's gait as they cross and placing them in a rather precarious position. If they do not have the required momentum to carry them over the threshold, they may become stuck in the liminal state of in between long enough to lose their balance.

When research students are stuck for extended periods of time and may also 'lose their balance', liminal states can be problematic. This is evident in the difficulties experienced by research students during the development of conceptual and theoretical frameworks, research paradigms, the central thesis argument, original knowledge creation, and data analysis (Kiley, 2009; Kiley & Wisker, 2008). In analyzing Aleta's PhD v.1.0 journey, she experienced extended liminal periods especially in the conceptualization of her project and the issues she experienced presenting a viable research proposal. These issues caused her difficulties in passing through the threshold from probationary status to fully confirmed candidate. In Aleta's case, supervisory style and institutional support, that did not fully meet her needs or align with her learning approach, were further impediments in the process.

Aleta's experiences highlight how threshold concepts and liminal states can be better identified, and the strategies students, supervisors, and institutions can employ to ensure the timely and successful navigation through any sticking points. For

Aleta, significant others, including personal networks, work colleagues, and research networks, were vital in assisting her to pass through transitional thresholds. Through engaging with other researchers outside of her supervisory team, during PhD v.1.0 and especially during PhD v.2.0, Aleta was able to successfully pass through her threshold moments and find her way as an effective researcher.

Peer networks are an important element in the traversal of threshold periods during the student research journey (Kiley, 2009) and more broadly in the context of academic career trajectory development (Heffernan, 2021). This is because networks provide a scaffolded enculturation into specific research cultures and the associated ways of doing things (Kiley, 2009). Students can engage with the network moving at their own pace from the periphery of the group (e.g., initial engagement, observing and participating in group activity) to the core (e.g., full group member, assuming core responsibilities in the group). This draws on the ideas of Legitimate Peripheral Participation (Lave & Wenger, 1991) and in the context of the research student journey, enables students to gradually and safely assume the necessary identities associated with researcher development (Kiley, 2009).

This type of scaffolded learning approach is not exclusive to peer networks and can also be achieved within the student's supervisory team. And so, there are additional benefits to networking and seeking supplementary researcher support outside of the supervisory team. Aleta's story highlights these clearly and provides another layer of support for peer networking as a means for students to transition through learning thresholds and liminal states more effectively. This is because it empowers the student with their own agency to select support from a variety of options (and people) within the network. In this way, the student is more likely to seek support from peers and significant others that closely aligns with their needs and learning approaches. If these networking opportunities are scaffolded into the research student journey, it provides an added level of support so that students do not lose their balance when crossing the threshold. The results of this approach mean that students can be assisted through the bitter and move on more quickly to enjoy the sweet.

3.4.2 Liminality, Significant Events and Affect

Doctoral research as a rite of passage is not only a cognitively challenging one but also an emotionally intensive experience (Cotterall, 2013) at varied levels and stages of the journey (Corcelles et al., 2019) and marked by significant events (Weise et al., 2020). Studies continue to affirm the role of emotions in student learning (Eynde & Turner, 2006; Linnenbrink-Garcia & Pekrun, 2011), it being an integral part of the doctoral experience as students learn to manage their emotional responses to significant events throughout the journey. Significant events include a range of important or critical activities, including cumulative happenings (McAlpine et al., 2009). As such, the discussion in this section analyzes Aleta's emotional dispositions during significant doctoral events beginning with cognitive and emotional dissonance and concluding with harmony in the end. Like all stories that result in resolution, the meanings behind the bitter and the sweet and their place in the journey are discussed.

In Aleta's case, cognitive dissonance was demonstrated by sustained workplace learning, the informal (as described in Chap. 2) versus a failure to progress in her doctoral study, the formal learning (as revealed in this chapter). The widening of research interests due to varied engagements in her university of employment was a positive occurrence; however, this had a negative effect on the acceptance of Aleta's research proposal conceptualizations as they had shifted away from her doctoral coursework area of study (curriculum development) and gravitated toward new areas as she indulged in emerging questions and understanding new-found theoretical frames (e.g., distance education). While this should be viewed as a form of growth, certain institutional requirements can pose a limitation especially when traditional doctoral programs only cater for specific areas and specialized original contributions as discussed in Chap. 1. We argue that this type of approach can restrict student learning, and although we agree that institutional structures are necessary it is important that these guide and nurture each student's individual journey rather than arbitrarily block alternate approaches.

The cognitive dissonance in Aleta's context took place under the setting of one main university system, where the residential campus represented the unsuccessful outcome of formal learning, and the online/virtual learning campus represented a new strand of research interest taking root. In each subsetting however, Aleta maintained affinity with the university's overall mission of the pursuit of academic excellence. The shared values of excellence and service to the nation were an apparent motivation to persist in thinking, rethinking, and knowledge building on a possible research area and contribution.

Emotional dissonance was unfolding in this background of cognitive dissonance. During particular experiences as a doctoral student negative feelings and realizations surfaced for Aleta as she came to terms with her own learning difficulties, triggered by significant events in her personal and professional life. Emotional dissonance emerged as feelings of inadequacy, isolation, and rejection negatively affected her ability to proceed with the next phase of her doctoral research. At the same time, she experienced feelings of satisfaction and confidence through professional growth (Chap. 2) and a sense of belonging as an academic within her open university of employment. The need to cope with these feelings and thoughts borne out of conflicting experiences within one university system as well as simultaneous and significant events, resulted in frustration and exhaustion. This was on top of the pressure she placed on herself to maintain a work-life balance.

Hence, Aleta's liminal phase of transitioning from the doctoral coursework to the doctoral thesis happened midlife with other significant events. The feelings of anger and self-blame had an effect on her confidence levels, similarly to how Templeton (2019) described depression as a doctoral student coming from a "self-perceived inability to solve issues within my professional, educational and personal spaces" (p. 399). Getting stuck in such a liminal state (Wisker et al., 2010) served to sink her into further depression. Hence, the doctoral experience is an actual challenge to one's capacity to make sense of both the positive and negative experiences and its accompanying roller coaster of emotions (Morrison-Saunders, et al., 2010) which can impact on one's confidence in the attainment of academic and personal goals.

3.4.3 Personal Agency and Affect

Weise et al. (2020) have revealed doctoral students experiencing a range of emotions triggered by significant events in their research journey, classified as events relating to the "academic community, the research process, research communication, personal agency and personal life" (p. 309). While heightened emotional experiences among doctoral students were reported as primarily surrounding the research process and communication, there were less significant events surrounding personal agency and personal life (Weise et al., 2020). In Aleta's case, however, it was a convolution of significant events in the research process and personal life that had an effect on her personal agency. One's sense of agency is affected by emotions and thus may vary throughout the journey (McAlpine & Amundsen, 2018b).

While this chapter affirms agency and affect as closely linked in one's identity trajectory as doctoral students, it also demonstrates how the resolution of tensions brought about by significant events, may also be found in one's personal agency and personal life (Weise et al., 2020). The decision to persist with the doctoral journey despite the challenging personal circumstances was highly influenced by Aleta's view of the teaching profession as a life choice grounded on the beliefs and values of education and nationalism. These were ideals she shared with her husband and fellow teacher-friends in her progressive school as detailed in Chap. 1, and now with university colleagues, all of whom were bound by a collective identity of being proud graduates of their beloved university. While there was no external validation from her university of study where her research proposal presentations were rejected, internal validation was gained through assurances from her significant others situated in her personal and professional networks. Aleta's unique and simultaneous experiences as a parent, a teacher, and an academic were a source of her personal agency and thus a great motivation to persist. Though significant events in her journey resulted in an eventual exit from the PhD v.1.0, a deeper sense of agency gave way to exploring other avenues to continue with her journey and the attainment of personal and academic goals through PhD v.2.0.

3.4.4 Becoming and Significant Others

The doctoral journey likened to a rite of passage as described by Kiley (2008) occurs through the stages "separation from one's known state, entering a state of liminality, and culminating in a 'becoming' that is marked by symbolism and ritual" (p. 57). The onset of Aleta's "becoming" entailed the ritual of exiting her PhD v.1.0, accepting the painful reality of giving up on her university in order to take her chances someplace else. There may have been severance of ties from the university of study but not in terms of valued relationships or collegial ties forged in her university of employment. This affirms the observation of being surrounded by peers or significant others in the researcher's learning environment as aiding the oscillation from a liminal state toward learning and transformation (Kiley, 2009). The result was Aleta opening up to the possibility of becoming an international student at a university outside of her country that aligned more closely with her student needs.

Aleta's identity trajectory amidst her doctoral journey affirms the role of personal networks (McAlpine & Amundsen, 2018a), that is relating with significant others as a valuable source of emotional support and encouragement (Douglas, 2020). Significant others are understood as one's life partner and family members but in some cases these include closest friends, colleagues, and others who bear influence on one's identity (Boylorn & Orbe, 2014). In the doctoral journey, personal and intellectual networks may be forged through a community of practice where experts engage to purposely contribute knowledge (Wenger, 1998). Alternatively, these networks have been observed to develop as doctoral students negotiate their interactions with peers and different groups at varied points throughout their journey (Douglas, 2020) likened to a form of peer learning arising from "unsupportive teaching regimes" (Boud & Lee, 2005, p. 509).

Thus, in the absence of an ideal research supervision and a sound research process within the remit of the institutional structure, the role of significant others, as an addition to the supervisory team are of prime importance. The challenge therefore lies in how institutions can not only improve research supervision but also expand the student's support network to include collegial and working relationships with support staff and other researchers (i.e., students and academic staff), with the understanding that "Candidates are engaged in 'learning the rules' but not in any didactic manner but rather by participating with peers and others within the environment. Through participation it is likely that newcomers not only transform themselves but also transform the group" (Kiley, 2008, p. 58). Through this approach students are more adequately supported and can be a source of support for others through both the bitter and the sweet aspects of the research journey.

References

Anderson, T., Rourke, L., Garrison, R. D., & Archer, W. (2001). Assessing teaching presence in a computer conferencing context. *Journal of Asynchronous Learning Networks, 5*(2), 1–17. https://doi.org/10.24059/olj.v5i2.1875

Beasy, K., Emery, S., & Crawford, J. (2021). Drowning in the shallows: An Australian study of the PhD experience of wellbeing. *Teaching in Higher Education, 26*(4), 602–618. https://doi.org/10.1080/13562517.2019.1669014

Boud, D., & Lee, A. (2005). Peer learning' as pedagogic discourse for education. *Studies in Higher Education, 30*(5), 1–17. https://doi.org/10.1080/03075070500249138

Boylorn, R. M., & Orbe, M. P. (Eds.). (2014). *Critical autoethnography: Intersecting cultural identities in everyday life.* Routledge. https://doi.org/10.4324/9781315431253

Brownlow, C., Eacersall, D., Nelson, C. W., Parsons-Smith, R. L., & Terry, P. C. (2022). Risks to mental health of higher degree by research (HDR) students during a global pandemic. *PLoS ONE, 17*(12), e0279698. https://doi.org/10.1371/journal.pone.0279698

Buirski, N. (2021). Liminal emotions and mindfulness traits of well-regarded supervisors in highly valued doctoral supervisory relationships. *SN Social Sciences, 1*(2), 1–18. https://doi.org/10.1007/s43545-020-00049-7

Corcelles, M., Cano, M., Liesa, E., González-Ocampo, G., & Castelló, M. (2019). Positive and negative experiences related to doctoral study conditions. *Higher Education Research & Development, 38*(5), 922–939. https://doi.org/10.1080/07294360.2019.1602596

Cotterall, S. (2013) More than just a brain: emotions and the doctoral experience. *Higher Education Research & Development, 32*(2), 174–187. https://doi.org/10.1080/07294360.2012.680017

Douglas, A. S. (2020). Engaging doctoral students in networking opportunities: a relational approach to doctoral study. *Teaching in Higher Education*, 1–17. https://doi.org/10.1080/13562517.2020.1808611

Eacersall, D. (2018). Quest for student success: An exploration of the academic skill needs of Higher Degree by Research students at a regional university. University of Southern Queensland. https://research.usq.edu.au/item/q74y8

Encarnacion, A. (2017, October 18). For the nation, for the people. *UP Forum.* https://up.edu.ph/for-the-nation-for-the-people/

Eynde, P. O., & Turner, J. E. (2006). Focusing on the complexity of emotion issues in academic learning: A dynamical component systems approach. *Educational Psychology Review, 18*, 361–376. https://doi.org/10.1007/s10648-006-9031-2

Guthrie, S., Lichten, C., van Belle, J., Ball, S., Knack, A., & Hofman, J. (2017). Understanding mental health in the research environment: A rapid evidence assessment. In *RAND Europe, Royal Society and the Wellcome Trust.* https://royalsociety.org/~/media/news/2017/understandingmental-health-in-the-research-environment.PDF

Heffernan, T. (2021). Academic networks and career trajectory: 'There's no career in academia without networks.' *Higher Education Research and Development, 40*(5), 981–994. https://doi.org/10.1080/07294360.2020.1799948

Keefer, J. M. (2015). Experiencing doctoral liminality as a conceptual threshold and how supervisors can use it. *Innovations in Education and Teaching International, 52*(1), 17–28. https://doi.org/10.1080/14703297.2014.981839

Kiley, M. (2008). Rites of passage and playing the doctoral game. In M. Kiley and G. Mullins (Eds.), *Quality in postgraduate research: research education in the new global environment* (pp. 56–60). The Centre for Educational and Academic Methods, The Australian National University. http://www.qpr.edu.au/Proceedings/QPR_Proceedings_2008.pdf#page=65

Kiley, M. (2009). Identifying threshold concepts and proposing strategies to support doctoral candidates. *Innovations in Education and Teaching International, 46*(3), 293–304. https://doi.org/10.1080/14703290903069001

Kiley, M., & Wisker, G. (2008, June). *'Now you see it, now you don't': Identifying and supporting the achievement of doctoral work which embraces threshold concepts and crosses conceptual thresholds.* Paper presented at Threshold Concepts: From Theory to Practice, Queen's University, Kingston, Ontario, Canada.

Lave, J. & Wenger, E. (1991). *Situated learning: Legitimate peripheral participation.* Cambridge University Press.

Linnenbrink-Garcia, L., & Pekrun, R. (2011). Students' emotions and academic engagement: Introduction to the special issue. *Contemporary Educational Psychology, 36*(1), 1–3. https://doi.org/10.1016/j.cedpsych.2010.11.004

Meyer, J., & Land, R. (Eds.). (2006). Threshold concepts and troublesome knowledge: An introduction. In *Overcoming barriers to student understanding: Threshold concepts and troublesome knowledge* (pp. 3–18). Routledge. https://doi.org/10.4324/9780203966273-9

McAlpine, L., & Amundsen, C. (2018a). Identity-trajectories of early career re-searchers. *Palgrave Macmillan.* https://doi.org/10.1057/978-1-349-95287-8

McAlpine, L., & Amundsen, C. (2018b). Structure and agency revisited (Chapter 4). In *Identity-trajectories of early career researchers* (pp. 57–70). Palgrave Macmillan. https://doi.org/10.1057/978-1-349-95287-8_4

McAlpine, L., Jazvac-Martek, M., & Hopwood, N. (2009). Doctoral student experience in education: Activities and difficulties influencing identity development. *International Journal for Researcher Development, 1*(1), 97–112. https://doi.org/10.1108/1759751x201100007

Morrison-Saunders, A., Moore, S. A., Hughes, M., & Newsome, D. (2010). Coming to terms with research practice: Riding the emotional rollercoaster of doctoral research studies. In M. Walker and P. Thompson (Eds.), *the routledge doctoral supervisor's companion* (pp. 224–236). Routledge. https://doi.org/10.4324/9780203851760

Shea, P., Hayes, S., Smith, S. U., Vickers, J., Bidjerano, T., Pickett, A., Gozza-Cohen, M., Wilde, J., & Jian, S. (2012). Learning presence: Additional research on a new conceptual element within the Community of Inquiry (CoI) framework. *The Internet and Higher Education, 15*(2), 89–95. https://doi.org/10.1016/j.iheduc.2011.08.002

Templeton, R. (2019). Depression, doctorates and self. In T. M. Machin, M. Clara, & P. A. Danaher (Eds.), *Traversing the doctorate* (pp. 393–407). Palgrave Macmillan. https://doi.org/10.1007/978-3-030-23731-8_3

Turner, V. (1977). Process, system, and symbol: a new anthropological synthesis. *Daedalus, 106*(3), 61–80. http://www.jstor.org/stable/20024494

Ugnayan ng Pahinungod (2000). *Buhay G.P., tatak U.P.* Ugnayan ng Pahinungod Diliman, University of the Philippines.

Villanueva, J. A. R. (2010a, December 1). From a dear colleague. *Scratch paper: Scratch paper: Aleta's evolving quests, confusions and equilibrium.* https://thisisgettingitchy.blogspot.com/2010/12/from-sol.html

Villanueva, J. A. R. (2010b, December 28). Letting the mud settle. *Scratch paper: Scratch paper: Aleta's evolving quests, confusions and equilibrium.* https://thisisgettingitchy.blogspot.com/2010/12/letting-mud-settle.html

Villanueva, J. A. R. (2012, December 21). Thesis...anti-thesis, and so I go on this way. *Scratch paper: Scratch paper: Aleta's evolving quests, confusions and equilibrium.* https://thisisgettingitchy.blogspot.com/2012/12/thesisanti-thesis-and-so-i-go-on-this.html.

Villanueva, J. A. R. (2014a, April 10). Thesis 2-2B dragonfly mode! *Scratch paper: Scratch paper: Aleta's evolving quests, confusions and equilibrium.* https://thisisgettingitchy.blogspot.com/2014/04/theses-2-2bdragonfly-mode.html

Villanueva, J. A. R. (2014b). Exploring ICT's and platforms for eLearning with K-7 learners: A seedbed for a prospective open high school program. In S. Jena, K. Agarwal, & S. K. Mahapatra (Eds.), *ICT in education: Perspectives on open and distance learning.* National Institute of Open Schooling, Noida. Shipra Publications.

Villanueva, J. A. R. (2019, November 15). *Research journey: A tale from the backend.* [Paper presentation]. 24th Postgraduate and Early Career Research Symposium, University of Southern Queensland, Toowoomba, Australia.

Villanueva, J. A. R. (2021, March 18). *PhD v.1.0 ~ v.2.0: A tale from the backend.* [Webinar]. EDUkussion Research Journeys II: The Birthing of Research Ideas and Theses Topics, University of the Philippines Open University Faculty of Education, Philippines. https://fed.upou.edu.ph/research-journeys-2/

Weise, C., Aguayo-González, M., & Castelló, M. (2020). Significant events and the role of emotion along doctoral researcher personal trajectories. *Educational Research, 62*(3), 304–323. https://doi.org/10.1080/00131881.2020.1794924

Wenger, E. (1998). *Communities of practice: Learning, meaning, and identity.* Cambridge University Press.

Wisker, G., Morris, C., Cheng, M., Masika, R., & Warnes, M. (2010). *Doctoral learning journeys: Final report.* The Higher Education Academy. https://www.heacademy.ac.uk/system/files/doctoral_learning_journeys_final_report_0.pdf

Part II

Ph.D. Version 2.0 ~ Ingress to Egress

Chapter 4
Enablers

Abstract In this chapter we use the Community of Inquiry (CoI) framework to analyze the positive experiences of an international student at an Australian university. Personal reflections and discussion of the CoI concepts of social presence, teaching presence, and cognitive presence demonstrate the benefits of positive research cultures for the development of productive research communities that support research student training and success. Two main groups, the Library Research Support Team and the Postgraduate and Early Career Research (PGECR) group as well as associated activities such as research writing bootcamps and research support consultations, are discussed as examples of initiatives to build these types of cultures. Within this environment students can increase their knowledge and skills to complete the research and extend their networks and mechanisms for support, outside of their supervisory team. We discuss the need for stakeholders to understand research as a developmental process and as a collaborative act of learning community building. In this way, research is not a lone experience for students, nor an experience only shared with supervisors, but is one of research community. We demonstrate the benefits of this, including a sense of self and belonging, multiple failsafe mechanisms of support, and increased provision to identify and meet student learning needs. In developing this approach, we argue that institutions, research supervisors, and research students should form a learning alliance to ensure mutual responsibility for learning success, but institutions bear the responsibility for developing and maintaining supportive research cultures and for ensuring that students have the knowledge and learning opportunities to engage in the alliance in productive and appropriate ways.

Keywords Doctoral Education · Research student · Student experience · Student success · Researcher identity · Higher Degree by Research · HDR · Postgraduate Research · PGR · Learning alliance · Community of Inquiry · CoI · Research supervision

MONDAY, APRIL 3, 2017

I came around to asking my Research Supervisor a question, then of course, she managed to see through what I was trying to word into an actual research question.

It practically opened what I can only label as My Can of Stars (and with the tune from Coldplay playing in the background) -- you can literally see me having stars surrounding my head, not out of a bad bump, but more out of sheer excitement with this new study I am treading on... and neatly seeing how it is a continuation of prior curiosities.

So, I'd like to capture this moment, knowing that at some point, the stars may become dark clouds of confusion or a mud of messiness... let that take care of itself.

Given that in a specific context such as learning communities in transition, there are clear cut/ defined roles among teachers and learners. But then possibly, there may exist shared roles in the area of social presence and sense of community. What if through my study, I initially capture the educational experiences of learners through the elements of the Community of Inquiry framework (CoI): "What is the nature of the educational experiences of learners in the Open High School programs?"

How about, I re-examine and investigate the elements of the CoI, particularly the development and interaction of the teaching presence (TP) and social presence (SP), or its overlap "setting the climate for learning". Upon the development of a virtual community site for open high school teachers and learners, what will be the manifestations of TP and SP in setting the climate for learning? How do these contribute to specific outcomes—such as sense of community or self-efficacy or even initial cognitive presence (CP)?

Maybe then, a reinterpretation of the CoI framework/model will emerge, if not additional indicators of it, or perhaps a rearrangement of the elements will take place to fit the context of learning communities in transition. This is like a prequel version of the CoI which may be applied at the secondary level, and in support of transitioning towards the direction of a more genuine CoI at the higher education level. Therefore, my study asks: In what ways can the CoI framework be utilized to examine the educational experiences of teachers and learners of the Open High School in the Philippines? (Villanueva, 2017a)

Aleta: At this time, I had been accepted into an international doctoral student program at a regional university in Australia. My prior immersions in K-12 pedagogy and practice as a teacher, in varied settings, as well as engagements in community development work, and then later on with virtual communities and blended learning platforms, evolved into an initial research topic (Fig. 4.1). My central research question asked, "In what ways do interactions and experiences of K-12 teachers and students indicate learning communities as outcomes of blended learning classes?" My subquestions raised: (1) what is the nature of interactions in the blended learning classes; (2) how are teaching presence, social presence, and cognitive presence manifested by teachers and students in their blended learning classes; and (3) how is learning community experienced by teachers and students in their blended learning classes (Villanueva, 2017b)?

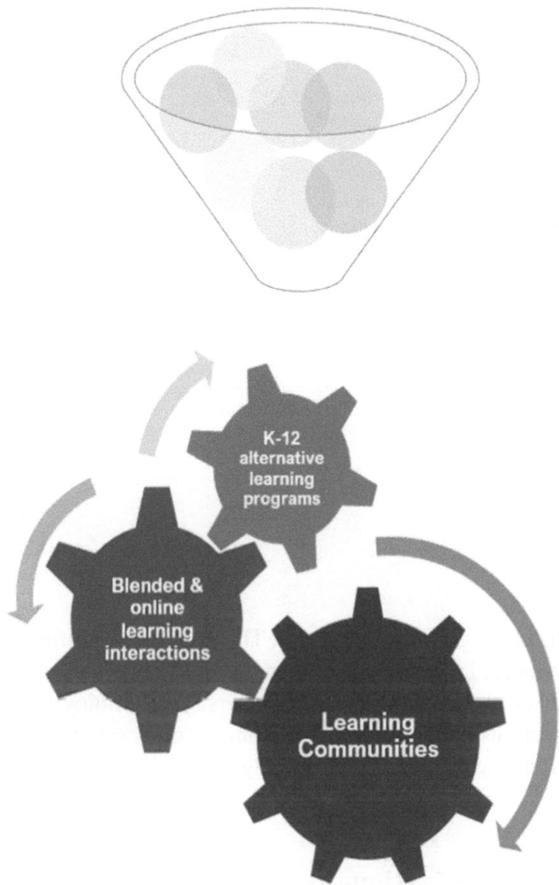

Fig. 4.1 Aleta's research areas as of April 2017. *Note.* From Aleta's confirmation of candidature presentation, Villanueva (2017b, December 6)

4.1 Enablers

Aleta: In this part, I now examine my educational experiences as an academic in an open university given the opportunity to undertake further studies both externally and on-campus, at this Australian university, through a doctoral study grant. In this chapter we use the Community of Inquiry (CoI) framework (Fig. 4.2) to analyze my interactions with significant others from both of these universities, face-to-face, and online. The discussion incorporates interactions with key individuals and teams who have made my journey colorful, educative, and most of all, coherent.

Within the presences of the CoI framework, indicators of social presence and cognitive presence include open communication, collaboration, critical discourse, and reflection on the process of learning (Garrison & Akyol, 2015; Garrison et al., 2001; Redmond, 2014). My doctoral thesis in the K-12 setting validated prior findings of the presences in higher education, that is, a strong social presence is positively

linked to cognitive presence. This is likewise affirmed through my educational experiences, informally and formally in the two universities—my Australian university
of doctoral study and my university of employment in the Philippines. The next
sections juxtapose findings from my doctoral thesis, which used the CoI framework
as a theoretical lens, to investigate my doctoral experiences.

4.2   Navigations at an Australian University: Cognitive Presence and Social Presence

Aleta: Cognitive presence and social presence, two elements from the CoI framework served to underpin my educational experiences as a provisional research
student moving toward becoming a fully confirmed PhD candidate. In higher education research, cognitive presence is examined through the practical inquiry cycle
with indicators of sense of puzzlement, information exchange, and connecting and
applying ideas (Garrison, 2017). Social presence is examined through indicators of
collaboration, group cohesion, and open communication (Garrison, 2017).

At my Australian university, the cognitive presence was felt through varied
engagements made available to research students in order to initiate them into the
research culture of the university. These learning opportunities were largely driven
by two groups which I tapped into at different phases of my PhD v.2.0—the Research
Support Team and the Postgraduate and Early Career Researcher (PGECR) group.

Of interest were distinct research events spread throughout the schoolyear which
I chanced upon during my on-campus stints and were recommended by my Research

Supervisor. During my first year, I was advised to consult with Douglas, the Learning Advisor, Higher Degree by Research (HDR), and engage in a workshop called The Research Writing Bootcamp. The workshop brought together HDR students and expert researchers to engage in writing and peer learning. The workshop introduced me to the Library Research Support Team and the valuable role the team plays in the lives of research students.

BLOG POST: GRRRRRAPES!

SUNDAY, NOVEMBER 12, 2017

Had my first taste of those grrrrapes at the Research Writing Bootcamp.

I didn't realize it could be that juicy.

At Day 1, were worthwhile exchanges with new-found superfriends all coming from our own causes and convictions, and the common drive to make something out of those. Within a few hours of Day 2 everything just fell into place. Collaboration as I've shared with willing listeners in my small group, entails seeing each other's strengths and limitations and having the willingness to engage in the process because of a shared goal to learn and contribute. It's simply about laying down your weapons, taking off your armor to see each other's real skin for all its moles, freckles, bumps, wrinkles and colors. Beneath the skin, your mates are struggling as you are, and keeping strong as you are. And in each other, we can only find an ally --- a coach, a cheering squad, an invigilator or someone with another pair of eyes trying to make sense of your writing.

So, here's the juice: I've got a pack of great feedback, quite honest and reassuring ones from my superfriends. I practically had no need to see Batman [pseudonym for Douglas] though I shall demand F2F coach time to experience the how-to & gain skills in helping my future research advisees.

Here at the university, I'm not just a student statistic so I shall continue to rely on E-Mode's [pseudonym for research librarian] words that they are here to help. I can only feel gratitude for the Research Support Team. At the sight of grapes or the taste of grape juice, you shall be remembered. (Villanueva, 2017b)

Douglas: Writing groups can take many forms. There are the shut up and write formats that focus on 'writing time' more than 'discussion time,' and there are more interactive models that integrate extensive learning and networking activities into the 'writing time'. The Research Writing Bootcamp tries to strike a balance between these two and provide participants with dedicated time to work on research and writing tasks as well as opportunities to engage with other researchers and specialized support staff. As experienced by Aleta, the benefits of writing groups are that they provide time and space for writing to be done with others. Writing and many of the processes of research can be difficult and lonely activities. The social nature of writing groups allows for a sense of accountability to the group and for difficulties and achievements to be shared. These activities provide social presence and the development of a sense of shared community and contribute to participants' cognitive presence through the sharing of ideas and collaborative feedback on writing exercises. This collaborative work not only assists in improving participant's writing but also generates discussions and thinking about the conceptualization and development of their research project. I would encourage all researchers to seek out a suitable writing group. If a student's institution does not have one, then I suggest they start their own. There are many online resources that can help with this.

Aleta: Cognitive presence and social presence were also felt through learning interactions facilitated by the Postgraduate and Early Career Researcher (PGECR) group under the leadership of Dr. P (pseudonym) and other academics at my Australian university. The PGECR bi-monthly meetings and biannual symposium served as venues for me to immerse in the collaborative learning culture at my new university. My sense of community with fellow doctoral students and researchers was forged through the sharing of resources and reflections, and especially through viewing practice Confirmation of Candidature presentations.

The PGECR meetings covered a range of topics: research methodologies, podcasting, autoethnography, expressions of gratitude, and most importantly effective research supervision. Facilitating discourse through peer learning as a form of teaching presence was embedded in these interactions, likened to a Community of Practice among research experts and research students with a shared goal of becoming effective researchers in a non-threatening, informal, and democratic way. One memorable PGECR meeting was for the group to engage in reflecting on our experiences of research supervision. Everyone was encouraged to define in concrete terms what good research supervision was (Fig. 4.3). I explicitly stated: (1) strategic communication; (2) establishing sense of connectedness; (3) timely sharing of content and resources; and (4) emphasis on research as collaborative act.

While the PGECR meetings deepened discussions on a range of experiences, issues, and concerns regarding what it means to engage in a research project, the PGECR symposium became a venue to appreciate a wide range of research topics coming from researchers within the university.

Blog Post: Post-PGECR Symposium

Saturday, 13 July 2019 @Scratch Paper Mahara

Of particular interest in the symposium were the varied presentations: lived experiences of cancer patients under clinical testing, research on the use of trans-language techniques in English as a Foreign Language among Japanese students, an HDR student's journey, yarning as an effective methodology among indigenous groups, data from PhD/HDR students and their reasons for getting into a PhD in the first place. I felt that I would have wanted 30 minutes just to listen to Dr. P and an HDR student who got curious with the color wheel. Best of all was the shared feeling of wanting to learn more from others' curiosities. Amazing how our minds work... and humbling experience to settle with what one is capable of understanding or embracing. We are not meant to know everything after all :). (Villanueva, 2019a)

In these PGECR experiences and sessions, my curiosities, concerns and ideas about research and the kind of research I would like to do felt right. Thus, listening and seeing others having similar questions and experiences served to validate and affirm my researcher identity. Within the cognitive presence of the CoI, indicators of puzzlement, information exchange, exploration of ideas and reflecting on content and

Fig. 4.3 Poster product from a PGECR session joined by Aleta. *Note.* Community of Practice—Research Supervision (CoP-RS), & Postgraduate and Early Career Researchers (PG&ECR) (Villanueva, 2019a, August 19). What are the essential ingredients for good soup-ervision? Used with permission

process were experienced (Garrison, 2017). These occurred alongside social presence indicators, namely, expression of emotion, self-disclosures, and most especially complementing and expressing appreciation (Garrison, 2017). These aligned with the characteristics of good 'soup-ervision' which I identified, having experienced this at my Australian university.

The elements and indicators of the CoI serve to understand online learning and collaboration in higher education research (Garrison et al., 2001). Intuitively, it helped me to appreciate my doctoral research journey, most especially the outcomes of my PhD v.2.0. One of which was research identity building. The research process and dissertation output were evidence of my layered identities, that of a K-12 teacher and an academic in higher education. This was not just any academic but an academic capable of substantial research. It was no longer just about dabbling in mini-case studies but rather a full-blown independent research project, more like an archeologist in a full-scale dig, and no longer a toddler in a sandbox of sorts.

4.3 Maximizing Student Support: Teaching Presence and Social Presence

Aleta: In my PhD v.2.0 project, teachers and students, within the K-12 setting, manifested roles of teaching presence as facilitators of learning. Students viewed their teachers as experts responsible for the design of content and activities, online and offline. At the same time, they saw themselves as being able to monitor their classmates' work and behavior or even serve as peer teachers helping to clarify topics and lessons. Students also anticipated face-to-face interactions to deepen their understanding of content under the direct instruction provided by their teachers. Students enacted their roles as 'eLearners' still wanting to engage as active listeners to their teachers. Teachers were transparent with their identities as individuals and/ or role models responsible for settling issues or conflicts among students, rapport-building, and sustaining connections with their students (Villanueva, 2021a, 2021b).

In the context of the student research experience, teaching presence and social presence were evident through my online and face-to-face interactions with key individuals at my new university. I gained the support I needed to be comfortable with my identity as an international doctoral student and a Filipino academic. Within these online exchanges are examples of these presences through direct instruction and facilitation provided by email (Figs. 4.4 and 4.5).

Aleta: Within the safety of my emails (Figs. 4.4, 4.5, and 4.6), I dared to bring up all sorts of questions and ideas, with more clarity of thought, and content ranging from work culture to qualitative data analysis, referencing, autoethnography, grammar, movies, and anything under the sun. These were types of questions which clutter up my brain which I could not manage to bring up during face-to-face PGECR meetings or online training sessions via Zoom.

I had ongoing email threads with key individuals from my Australian university in the same way I also kept ongoing conversations with my colleagues in my home university. The use of these types of pseudonyms (e.g., B-Wayne—Bruce Wayne, Spider-M—Spiderman) was reminiscent of being a junior faculty in my home university when I ascribed superhero names to my colleagues. I recall creating a page at my *Scratch Paper*, university of employment Google site, where I engaged my colleagues with questions as part of my 'getting to know' their interests and 3-year and 5-year plans as academics. Using my Australian university email, I carried over the same practice, which kept me afloat during the data analysis phase and up until the dissertation writing phase of my doctoral study.

Along with online communications were on-campus face-to-face opportunities for research students to engage in learning on our own and with others in varied spaces. There were the Research Bites series of online workshops attended by fellow research students. At several of these events, I joined with other international students and research supervisors to share our experiences regarding the institutional opportunities and resources to help students approaching their Confirmation of Candidature. Interaction with content was also made possible through the repository of learning objects where prior presentations on research writing are made accessible along with

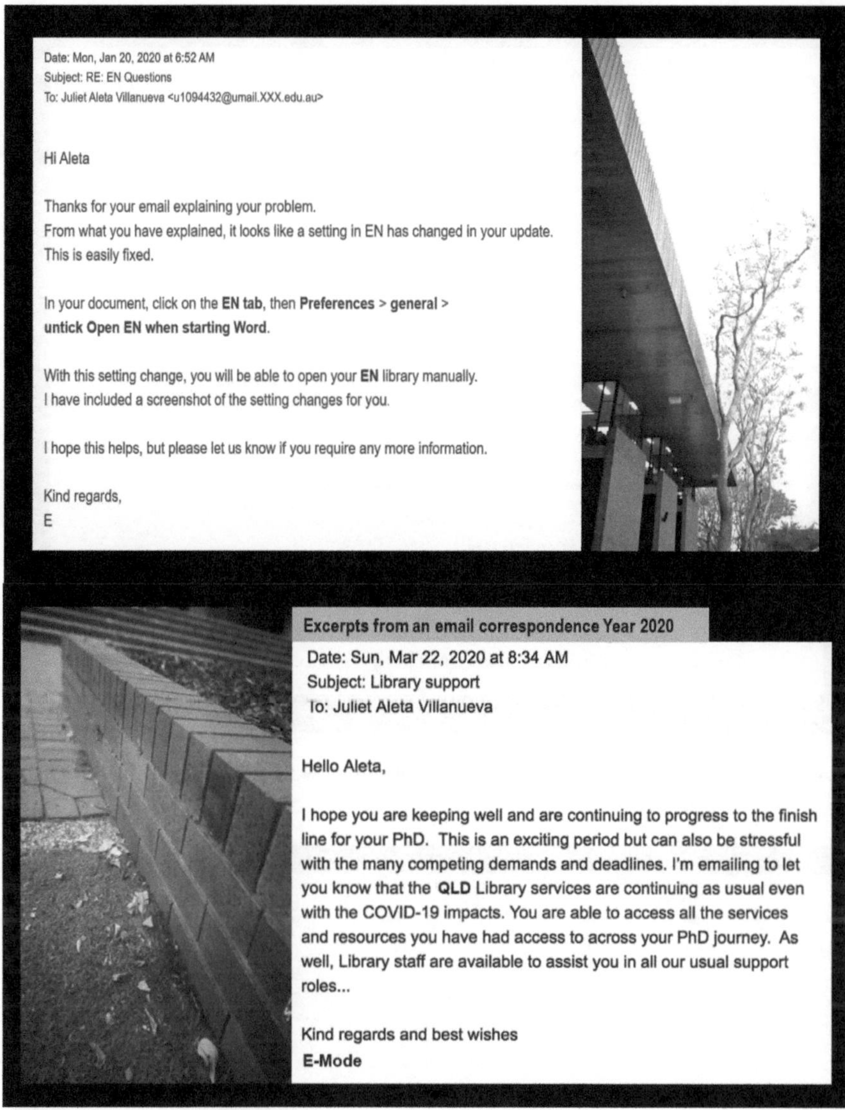

Fig. 4.4   A montage of email responses from the library research support team. *Note.* Adapted from Villanueva (2021b), "Becoming part of a collaborative learning culture"

tutorials for students on internet safety and security. Thus, a combination of these online and offline activities contributed to building a sense of community within my Australian university.

I was fortunate to be sponsored by my university of employment, so I was able to do a full study leave allowing for offline and face-to-face opportunities. I maximized being on-campus in Australia, by immersing myself in the learning culture and

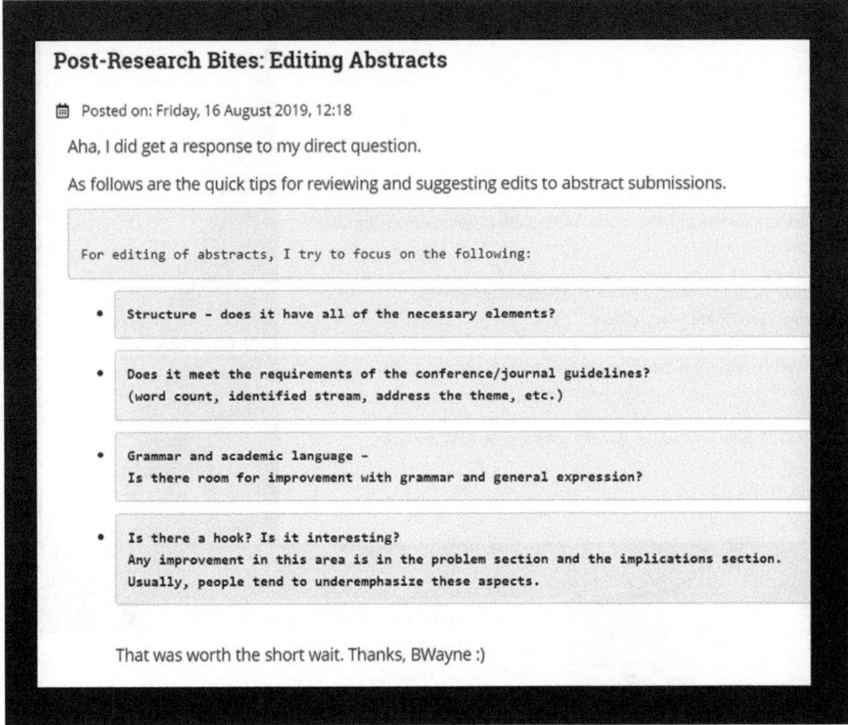

Fig. 4.5 Screenshot of Aleta's blog about an email response. *Note.* Adapted from Villanueva (2019b), Scratch Paper @Mahara

Fig. 4.6 Montage of Aleta's email subjects with key academics/staff. *Note.* A screenshot from email thread topics with key individuals (using pseudonyms) from Aleta's Australian university (own photo)

Fig. 4.7 Image of a social media post: the on-campus learning environment. *Note.* Montage of mobile phone pictures and social media posts by Villanueva (2019a, 2019b), from Facebook and Google reviews (own photos)

engaging in social interactions with fellow students and academics. All of a sudden, it felt as if 'my cup overfloweth'. Education in my Australian university filled my learning needs to the brim, like coffee from the Faculty of Education coffee machine. That was the only way I could describe my experiences of being truly understood and acknowledged for what I could do. It resulted in me posting comments through social media (Figs. 4.7 and 4.8).

As a member of the university community, I was glad to have the opportunity to reciprocate in more ways than one: (1) dutifully filling out feedback forms; (2) commenting or reviewing content for research student course materials; (3) sharing my experiences on the Confirmation of Candidature; (4) volunteering as a Digital Advisor providing feedback on the digital content at the university website; and (5) being part of the LGBTIQ support network. I realized that navigating my doctoral journey became a pleasurable experience given the dedicated time and supportive environment which allowed me to choose what and how I would learn.

In the past, I have experienced collaborative engagements with fellow academics in international collaborative book projects. These prior experiences entailed online interactions and critical discourse leading to attainment of shared goals—an eventual publication. The process however did not necessarily result in a sense of community or the feeling of connectedness and mattering defined by McMillan and Chavis (1986) which has been applied in higher education research (Librero, 2021; Rovai, 2002). My new-found educational experience in an Australian university has been significant given that it solidified my academic identity as a research student and PhD candidate, leading to my connectedness with faculty, other academic staff, and fellow doctoral students, and being truly part of an international learning community.

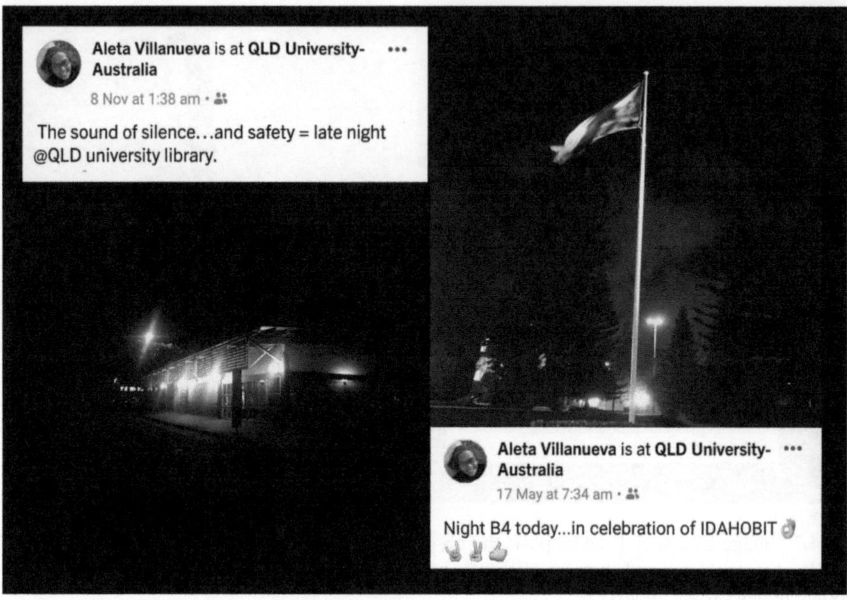

Fig. 4.8 Other social media posts: on-campus study in an Australian University. *Note*. Montage of mobile phone pictures and social media posts by Villanueva (2019a, 2019b), from Facebook and Google reviews (own photos)

Douglas: It is common for research students to express the need for more opportunities to engage with their peers and experience forms of social presence. This reflects a desire to share stories of undertaking research and to discuss their research with like-minded individuals. For this reason, we incorporate several online, face-to-face, and blended learning activities into our researcher development programs. These initiatives are designed to not only provide students with training in researcher skills but also opportunities to engage with other researchers and develop extended research networks outside of their supervisory team. These develop a real sense of community and opportunities for positive engagement with research students, research support staff, researchers, and research supervisors. As part of these learning events, students (and more experienced researchers) are encouraged to share their research experiences and understandings of the research process. It is evident in the experiences of Aleta that these types of activities are important in building research cultures based on shared experiences and purpose and a sense of community and belonging. Through a combination of social, cognitive, and teaching presence, they offer additional layers of support for research students to meet their learning needs more effectively than models which rely heavily on the supervisory team.

4.4 Research as Learning Community Building

The CoI framework, and its presences, has been used to examine and reflect on doctoral education as experienced in a blended learning mode. In higher education research, a collaborative learning community is one of the goals and outcomes of the framework. The framework has also been validated to investigate blended and online learning courses and other kinds of learning communities within distance education programs. Through reflection on, and analysis of, Aleta's research journey, research as learning community building has been uncovered in the context of research education experiences (Fig. 4.9).

Research as learning community building was evident in Aleta's interactions with key university experts, teams, and fellow HDR students as she experienced the processes involved in undertaking an independent research project externally and on-campus. The varied interactions revealed here served to strengthen Aleta's prior knowledge and skills on qualitative research while building her academic identity and connectedness within a learning community enabled by her Australian regional university. In sum, the positive research student experiences were borne out of Aleta's sense of community with members of her new-found academic networks resulting in a renewed confidence in herself. Sense of community was redefined by McMillan (2021) as:

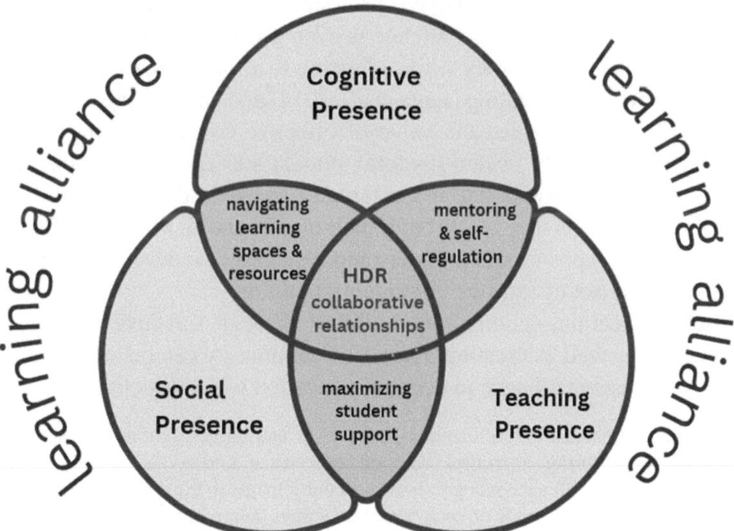

Fig. 4.9 Research as learning community building through the CoI Framework. *Note.* Adapted from "CoI Framework" by Garrison et al. (2000), (https://coi.athabascau.ca/coi-model/). With permission from the Community of Inquiry website and licensed under the CC-BY-SA International 4.0 license (https://creativecommons.org/licenses/by-sa/4.0/)

a spirit of belonging together, a feeling that there is an authority structure that can be trusted, an awareness that trade, and mutual benefit come from being together, and a spirit that comes from shared experiences that are preserved as art. (para. 2)

In this sense, the authority structure for Aleta was represented by the new-found university of study within which she, as the doctoral student, established trust toward the supervisory team and support staff. The resulting trade or exchange of resources, when undertaken properly, can benefit the university, fellow students, and academics. The art can take the form of expression of learning experiences shared through anecdotes, stories, and presentations for meetings and symposia. In essence, it is the sense of community in one's research journey which becomes a source of pleasure and positivity.

The experiences in an Australian university, as narrated in this chapter, equally highlight how institutional support mechanisms can position students to experience success in their research journey. In other words, a greater sense of agency and an intrinsic motivation to succeed, as in Aleta's case, was met halfway through institutions taking seriously their responsibilities to ensure quality research training and support services are made accessible (Emmerson, 2019). In Aleta's PhD v.1.0 the lack of institutional resource support was experienced in the university of study. Likewise, McAlpine and Amundsen (2016, 2018) indicated how doctoral students who are at the same time academics or in research-teaching positions have had negative experiences in the area of institutional resources and responsibilities while undertaking their doctoral study. This major gap has profound effects on any doctoral student's disposition for that matter. The challenge is even greater for international students engaged in their doctoral journey while adjusting to a foreign learning environment which could prove to be isolating (Janta et al., 2014) and challenging (Zhang, 2016). Emmerson (2019) highlighted the value of effective communication flows as an institutional responsibility toward doctoral student success. Hence, what doctoral students, especially international and externally based students, can initially rely on, are communications that get through their emails and links to useful university website pages and repositories to understand research as a developmental process and a collaborative act of learning community building.

Research as learning community building through effective and reciprocal communication as well as creating a sense of community can be understood using the concept of learning alliance in doctoral education which is defined as:

...the implicit agreement of each student, supervisor and university that they are jointly responsible for ensuring a fruitful doctoral experience and a high-quality doctoral degree...The learning alliance recognizes that all participants in the doctoral process bring resources to and make demands on each other but defines their relationship as a cooperative endeavor of reciprocal responsibilities and obligations. (Halse & Bansel, 2012, p. 384)

This means moving beyond the view of research supervisory relationships and monitoring proper delivery of institutional services and academic support in aid of the doctoral student. It is grounded on a mutual sense of responsibility, characteristic of building "true community" and "by design" (Peck, 2010, p. 59) making students, support staff, and supervisors equally work for the common good and likewise made accountable. This chapter asserts that a learning alliance at work in research education means that design, disposition, and strategy are grounded on the understanding that research entails a learning community building process which is intentional and agentive.

Likewise, it can be said that research study calls upon the student's skills in navigating and decision-making as well as attitudes of risk-taking and humility to accept that one needs help to get through the journey successfully. A greater sense of agency pushed Aleta to explore institutional resources within her university to finally arrive at a doctoral education program which afforded the flexibility and independence she seemed to be looking for at this stage in her life. This brave choice opened doors for her to benefit from the best fit academic support and research supervision attuned to her academic and learning needs. When examined through the metaphor of a doctoral journey, as revealed in this chapter, the surrounding events and actions, as well as engagements with significant others are equally valuable. Therefore, the personal, the incidental, and the intuitive are given due consideration. Certain aspects of the doctoral research journey are not exactly discerned by doctoral students at the start of the journey nor while in the thick of it. Only through the act of reflection can one fully realize the incidental discoveries, one of which is self-discovery and as such may vary from one doctoral student to the next. These variations, to a great extent, account for unique meanings derived from research relationships, identity development, and student success which are examined in the remaining chapters.

References

Emmerson, M. (2019). *Communicating 'success' with research students: Institutional responsibilities in encouraging a culture of research higher degree completions.* In T. M. Machin, M. Clara, & P. A. Danaher (Eds.), *Traversing the doctorate* (pp. 57–73). Palgrave Macmillan. https://doi.org/10.1007/978-3-030-23731-8_3

Garrison, D. R. (2017). *E-learning in the twenty-first century: A community of inquiry framework for research and practice.* Routledge.

Garrison, D. R., & Akyol, Z. (2015). Toward the development of a metacognition construct for communities of inquiry. *The Internet and Higher Education, 24*, 66–71. https://doi.org/10.1016/j.iheduc.2014.10.001

Garrison, D. R., Anderson, T., & Archer, W. (2000). CoI Framework. https://coi.athabascau.ca/coi-model/

Garrison, D. R., Anderson, T., & Archer, W. (2001). Critical thinking, cognitive presence, and computer conferencing in distance education. *American Journal of Distance Education, 15*(1), 7–23. https://doi.org/10.1080/08923640109527071

Halse, C., & Bansel, P. (2012). The learning alliance: Ethics in doctoral supervision. *Oxford Review of Education, 38*(4), 377–392. https://doi.org/10.1080/03054985.2012.706219

Janta, H., Lugosi, P., & Brown, L. (2014). Coping with loneliness: A netnographic study of doctoral students. *Journal of Further and Higher Education, 38*(4), 553–571. https://doi.org/10.1080/0309877X.2012.726972

Librero, A. F. D. (2021). Online student engagement and sense of community in a Philippine online university. *International Journal on Open and Distance E-Learning*, *7*(1). https://ijodel.com/index.php/ijodel/article/view/65

McAlpine, L., & Amundsen, C. (2016). Post-PhD career trajectories: Intentions, decision-making and life aspirations. *Palgrave Macmillan*. https://doi.org/10.1057/978-1-137-57660-6

McAlpine, L., & Amundsen, C. (2018). Identity-trajectory (Chapter 3). In *Identity-trajectories of early career researchers*, (pp. 27–56). Palgrave Macmillan. https://doi.org/10.1057/978-1-349-95287-8_3

McMillan, D. (2021). Sense of community. *Dr. David McMillan*. https://www.drdavidmcmillan.com/sense-of-community/sense-of-community

McMillan, D. W., & Chavis, D. M. (1986). Sense of community: A definition and theory. *Journal of Community Psychology, 14*(1), 6–23. https://doi.org/10.1002/1520-6629(198601)14:1%3c6::aid-jcop2290140103%3e3.0.co;2-i

Peck, M. S. (2010). *The different drum: Community making and peace*. Simon and Schuster.

Redmond, P. (2014). Reflection as an indicator of cognitive presence. *E-Learning and Digital Media, 11*(1), 46–58. https://doi.org/10.2304/elea.2014.11.1.46

Rovai, A. P. (2002). Building sense of community at a distance. *The International Review of Research in Open and Distributed Learning, 3*(1), 1–16. https://doi.org/10.19173/irrodl.v3i1.79

Villanueva, J. A. R. (2017a, April 3). My can of stars. *Scratch paper: Aleta's evolving quests, confusions and equilibrium*. https://thisisgettingitchy.blogspot.com/2017/04/my-can-of-stars-whats-ifs.html

Villanueva, J. A. R. (2017b, November 12). Grrrrrapes! *Scratch paper: Scratch paper: Aleta's evolving quests, confusions and equilibrium*. https://thisisgettingitchy.blogspot.com/2017/11/grrrrrapes.html

Villanueva, J. A. R. (2019a, July 13). Post-PGECR symposium. *Aleta's scratch Paper@Mahara*. https://eportfolio.usq.edu.au/user/aleta-villanueva/aleta-villanueva

Villanueva, J. A. R. (2019b, August 16). Post-research bites: Editing abstracts. *Aleta's Scratch Paper@Mahara*. https://eportfolio.usq.edu.au/user/aleta-villanueva/aleta-villanueva

Villanueva, J. A. R. (2021a). Teaching presence in K-12 blended learning programs under the alternative delivery mode. *International Journal of Online Distance and eLearning, 7*(1). University of the Philippines Open University and in collaboration with the Philippine Society for Distance Learning. https://ijodel.com/june-2021-issue/

Villanueva, J. A. R (2021b, August 31). *Becoming part of a collaborative learning culture at USQ*. [PowerPoint slides]. Research Supervisors Community of Practice Meeting. University of Southern Queensland.

Zhang, Y. L. (2016). International students in transition: Voices of Chinese doctoral students in a US research university. *Journal of International Students, 6*(1), 175–194. https://doi.org/10.32674/jis.v6i1.487

Chapter 5
No Turning Back

Abstract For research students, the thesis represents the crowning achievement of many years of work. This chapter covers the write up of the thesis with a specific focus on research as a collaborative relationship. Autoethnographic reflections of an international research student at an Australian university are analyzed to better understand the shape of positive relationships between students and supervisors and other support staff. Trust and respect are identified as significant aspects of positive research relationships. The importance of positive collaborative research relationships is outlined along with approaches to developing them in trusting and respectful ways. Self-determination theory, and its focus on the basic psychological needs of competence, social relatedness, and autonomy, is discussed as a viable approach to this. If this strategy is taken, then effective research relationships can be established and maintained. We argue that supervisors and support staff should be encouraged to use approaches such as this that facilitate research success and positive research journeys.

Keywords Doctoral Education · Research student · Student experience · Student success · Researcher identity · Higher degree by research, HDR · Postgraduate Research, PGR · Research supervision · Self-determination theory, SDT

BLOG POST: WHEN THE GOING GETS TOUGH…THE UNDERWOODS GET GOING

MONDAY, OCTOBER 9, 2017

My advisers thankfully have held on… as dutifully and as interestingly as they can. I say interestingly because I am amazed with their professionalism, capability, and kindness = the quality of mentoring I need at this time. This is me acknowledging that I need all the help I can get and YES, I can help myself.

What does my university education, the Australian kind mean to me now? It means my flaws are real as can be and I can face up to these. While in the midst of political turmoil, social decay, frustrating leadership in my home country under D'tardism which I have no control over, all I can do is solve ME. This way, I can solve what there is to be (Villanueva, 2017).

* * *

BLOG POST: 19TH MONTH NO TURNING BACK

24 SEPTEMBER 2018, ALETA'S SCRATCH PAPER@MAHARA

Officially approved by the University Ethics Committee just recently. My advisers helped through fine-tuning those connections. To them I am most grateful cuz it takes alternate versions of my favorite co-teacher [and husband], Teacher Vic to understand how this brain of mine operates.

Gaining the approvals were far from my thoughts when I was struggling to see my study clearly through my muddled brain. My ideas are always interwoven or hyperlinked to something else which maybe to some have no relation at all. Realizing this as a learner somehow made me understand more how my son thinks, and how other younger students actually think as they sort out ideas on their own and when they aren't ready to learn in the manner we want them to learn. Now even more, I am able to identify with their difficulties, while being an online learner myself wanting to challenge barriers to make my kind of learning happen (Villanueva, 2018).

5.1   Mentoring and Self-regulation: Cognitive Presence and Teaching Presence

Aleta: In the process of conceptualizing my research project, cognitive presence and teaching presence were felt through the mentoring approaches employed by my research supervisors. They guided me to decide on the breadth of my study through facilitating discussions and raising questions during scheduled supervisory meetings. Through information exchange of a curated set of readings sent by email, I was able to validate my prior understanding of research paradigms as well as experiences in qualitative case studies. The readings allowed me to explore the possibility of carrying out a mixed method approach through design-based research. Through pressing questions from my supervisory team, I was able to rule out that approach and get back on track with an exploratory qualitative case study approach for my research project.

My research supervisors' style of mentoring, which I describe as a combination of hands-on and hands-off approaches, seemed to be best fit for the kind of learning I have engaged in since my PhD v.1.0. A part of my learning process operates on intuition as a way of knowing. Sometimes, it takes a long and winding road. I spend time on the peripherals before I get to the core with moments behaving like a toddler distracted in a sandbox of sorts. The hands-off approach was necessary, so I could be left to sort things out on my own, knowing and trusting that I can still come out of it alive and thinking. The hands-on approach was often felt through valuable comments and feedback on my written work as I labored through my data analysis and initial chapter writing. Through their timely reminders and assurance, I have come to realize that my process is a valid one, the messy and the fuzzy included.

A significant realization at this stage was that my once small collegial circle solely occupied by colleagues from my university of employment had widened to include significant others from my Australian university of study. Dr. R and Dr.

Fig. 5.1 Research Supervisor Comment on Aleta's Progress AY 2019–2020. *Note.* Adapted from Villanueva (2020d), "Research journey v.2.0: Ingress to egress"

G, my research supervisors, were like faculty members who gave generous advice. Their mentoring also involved strategies to plan prospective publications and future research directions. This collegial relationship was shaped through sharing experiences where I felt included as a faculty member, and thus our academic identities became more transparent, making me feel as a coequal (Fig. 5.1).

Facilitating discourse and direct instruction, indicators of teaching presence, were likewise experienced through the hands-on mentoring in academic writing. Here, I had the best of both worlds, undertaking my doctoral study in a blended manner, externally, online, and on-campus. The consultations were in the form of face-to-face and online interactions with quality and timely feedback by email. My research supervisors consistently provided direct comments on my dissertation, like trusted birthing coaches patiently laboring through my drafts. They were able to identify the negative and positive aspects of my work which I could then rethink or further accentuate.

I maintained constant communication with key language and academic writing experts, through English Angels and the Learning Advisor for Higher Degree Researchers (HDR-LA), both of whom were highly recommended by my supervisor. Douglas, the coauthor of this book, was the HDR-LA. He affirmed what writing worked and called attention to areas that needed rethinking. Like a true comrade-in-arms, he listened and posed alternate perspectives in my battle to hurdle barriers and overcome difficulties. I also turned to an English Angel to give the HDR-LA and my supervisors some breathing space. Her generosity and empathy were felt through quality time spent on my written work and just-in-time nudges to move forward. Eventually, I regained trust and confidence in my own process as a researcher, knowing that I could rely on the relationships I had built with these key individuals from my Australian university.

BLOG POST: ZOOM 332057716 IN MY MIND

SUNDAY, JANUARY 26, 2020

Been getting all sorts of help from HDR-learning advisor for quite some time.

Yr 1: Got feedback on my initial literature review. The feedback/comments came across as cautious - quite polite. Very helpful.

Yr 2: An 'impression type' of feedback on a new section on Blended Learning in my literature review which resulted in a concise paper presentation at ICODEL 2018.

Then came Yr 3. What came were actual notes on my creative work as I was like 'oido-ing' (or playing it by ear in music), the how-to of an auto-ethnography. A great part of the experience is that I have an artifact of an actual handwritten set of comments and tips on my written expression as an HDR learner, me. That's my antennae responding to my need2learn-how2mentor future research advisees. The comments let me see the bigger picture while the nitty gritty corrections looked like decorations on my white sheets of paper.

Sandwiched in between months of being on-campus was time well spent with the academic from English Angels. She went very gently and carefully through my presentation of findings. She reiterated that writing requires deep thought – and she showed me how to look at my own work then explained her comments. Smooooth.

Topic sentence...support, support with details...give examples.

That's like a grade three lesson on main ideas and supporting details.

Then there's more:

String the phrases/terms to sustain the reader's attention.

Handhold your reader through your work.

Got some good stuff done:)

Now came the iLibCalendar [online consultation booking tool]. Let me just get those slots with HDR-LA! In return, were kind & encouraging words about the whole process of doing a PhD. Perhaps it was to cushion what else was there to come. A bunch of pressing questions. I'm getting repeated reminders to be explicit with my thesis arguments, and tougher questions to make me think beyond my chapter Discussion. This is to make sure I hit those WIIFM = so what's in it for me. (Villanueva, 2020a)

Among the mentioned mentors/collaborators, I consider the HDR-LA role most interesting. This is due to my background in special education and work with K-12 students having learning disabilities. While consulting with Douglas, I realized he was a tertiary level version of language and learning support teachers in my home country. In my small school, my husband and I conceptualized an integrated literacy support program wherein a teacher provides intervention and additional imbedded support to students in their classes. This way learning happens while engaged in the actual reading and writing in both language and content area subjects, hence literacy instruction taking place in the natural setting.

As I shifted to university work in my home country, I found that even at the tertiary level adult learners still needed academic language support, even for their written assignments. So, it was quite a neat surprise engaging with the HDR-LA, only this time, the tables had turned as I was the student clearly in need of support. At the tertiary level, I noticed that the HDR-LA role provided a well-rounded approach to address the varied concerns of research students, to include just-in-time sharing of knowledge and resources or what we in the K-12 area recognize as 'teachable' moments.

BLOG POST: A NEAT KIND OF NITPICKING

THURSDAY, FEBRUARY 20, 2020

Days later, I decided to schedule a consultation with Dr. D and try things differently. So, what if I compare my scores with the expert abstract writer-reviewer. Why not try to practice giving comments on my work, as if, I'm giving feedback to a student. Neat!

I felt at some point, the ideas in my abstract got too 'scattered'. Dr. D noticed that I could have driven important points more directly. And that one way to do that was to look at the wordings/key phrases in the actual description of conference themes, then use those in the abstract. Hardly did that before! (Villanueva, 2020b)

* * *

BLOG POST: IT'S LIKE THIS 3

WEDNESDAY, MAY 13, 2020

A bit of background:

In the process of writing my auto-ethno on my PhD journey, I have had quality exchanges with key persons engaged in providing research support and learning advice from my Australian university. This made me curious about the role of the HDR-LA. There is no such thing as an LA in my university [of employment]. I figured perhaps, if universities in the Philippines had more LAs, library support for researchers and working with Research Supervisors, perhaps we'd have more teachers completing their MAs and PhDs without further delay. So, how does one become an LA? How do you prepare one to become an LA? And more – what's in the 'make-up' of an existing LA expert. How can you actually engage them to un-pack what they know and what they are learning so that they can recommend ways other teachers or professionals can learn these too? (Villanueva, 2020c)

Hence, reflecting on my relationship building with Douglas as HDR-LA, the process was partly driven by curiosity to understand the expertise of a researcher development specialist and learning advisor and what I can learn from our exchanges to be able to translate it to my future mentoring in the area of academic writing among research students at my home university. Areas of strengths and weaknesses in my writing were pointed out by Douglas through direct comments on my work but within a climate of trust. It was helpful feedback minus the feeling of being graded or judged. I appreciated having another pair of eyes examining my work, clearly diagnosing areas that needed reworking, especially paragraphs which needed to communicate arguments more clearly. This process of engaging and responding to feedback shaped my critical thinking through research writing. In our one-on-one consultations, there was an acknowledgment of writing as messy and difficult, with him making mention of his own experiences as a doctoral student, and the way through it by simply continuing writing and rewriting.

During my dissertation writing stage, another writing group was organized and facilitated by Douglas. This was the Research and Writing League (RWL) where fellow research students met for two straight hours online, once a week, to share insights about writing and meet target outputs. Most of the members were also part of the Postgraduate and Early Career Researcher (PGECR) meetings which became a good way of tracking the development of each other's research projects.

"The Research Writing League has helped contain my panic and angsty moments nearing my deadlines" (Andersen, et al., 2021, p. 14). Overall, this was what the RWL meant to me during the dissertation writing phase of my journey. It also had other benefits as is evident in feedback I provided to Douglas via email after one of the RWL sessions:

> Given the short, protected time to write, I accomplished:
>
> > editing 2 paragraphs from my findings-analysis chapter AND
>
> > putting together proposed changes to an instrument I used in my research project.
>
> I appreciate the invitation and suggestion of 'writing with a group' as I realized that I can capitalize on the presence of others to get me going. And I learned that in the few instances that I got distracted (outside noise), I got back on track just by seeing others working quietly. Therefore, I think that the RWLeague or group writing activity is a good way to co-regulate. (Villanueva, personal communication, December 17, 2019)

Douglas: Aleta found at least three significant things during her Australian PhD journey. She found a circle of support in the form of supervisors and additional staff within the institution, which assisted her to find her topic and associated contribution to the field and to find herself as a developing and blossoming researcher. What this demonstrates is the importance of relationship building in the research process. Through Aleta's experiences it is clear that collaboration and teamwork play an important role in the research student journey. It is a difficult journey and significant others can assist the student to arrive at their destination more quickly, and in better shape, than if they had undertaken the journey alone. The building of rapport and nurturing from all parties is fundamental in establishing and continually developing these relationships. This is vital throughout all aspects of the journey but has particular significance at the beginning of the relationship and during intense periods of writing. In examining my interactions with Aleta through the process of this autoethnography, I have thought about how I, as a research supervisor and learning advisor, build relationships of trust. I believe it is through the building of rapport and particular methods of feedback on writing. If this trust can be established then research student confidence and identity can be shaped in positive ways.

There are many successful styles of supervision and approaches to learning support. From my own perspective, I find that collaborative approaches that place oneself beside the student on the journey are the most fruitful. Sharing one's own experiences and difficulties, as I did with Aleta, can be a good way to do this, as well as demonstrate empathy and an understanding of the difficulties students face. There must be a sincere desire for not only student success but to understand the student's needs (Eacersall, 2018) and provide options and learning so that the student can make informed decisions about their own direction. Active listening and dedicated ongoing engagement with the project are key elements in this process. The student-researcher can feel when these are in place, and the result is increased levels of trust within the relationship.

The research journey can be a difficult one especially during the stages of writing the thesis. This is because it is at this point that the findings and contribution of the work must become concrete elements on the page. It is also when the research student can more clearly identify if what they have is what they need to meet the requirements of the degree. Often, they find that they do not quite have it right, and adjustments need to be made and so the cycle of drafting and redrafting continues. Writing is representative of the project, and its merits laid bare for all to see. It represents the quality of the research, its significance, and ultimately the worth of the student as a researcher. The words on the page carry significant meaning for the student and their own view of their researcher identity and standing as contributor to the field. In this process, the delivery of feedback on writing is important. Feedback needs to be delivered in the right ways to ensure that trust within the research relationship is built and/or maintained. The person delivering the feedback needs to be very cognizant of the vulnerabilities the student may be feeling and tailor the feedback accordingly.

There are two parts to feedback, the content of the feedback and how that content is delivered. Supervisors and others involved in the written feedback process need to get both aspects right. The content needs to provide advice to the student that will improve their thesis and overall academic writing, and it needs to be delivered in a way that the student can easily understand and accept. I remember the times I have received feedback that was overly critical and alternatively the times it was delivered with a critical yet constructive tone. I think as supervisors and learning support advisors we must be wary of falling into the pattern of just pointing out everything that is wrong with the thesis. Of course, part of the job is pointing out issues and suggesting alternative ways of doing things, but this should be done in an empathetic and understanding way, and we must remember to also point out the positives. It is only through identification of these that the student can understand them and continue to produce them in the thesis. As experienced by Aleta, constructive feedback delivered in positive ways builds confidence and capability and plays a role in developing and sustaining trust within the research relationship.

5.2   Research as a Collaborative Relationship

Research relationships have been examined in prior studies in terms of collaborative research teams where academics and graduate-level students are relegated into smaller research groups working closely with each other and their supervisors (Tobin, 2007). Positive emotional energy and solidarity have been reported as by-products of successful engagements among research teams (Ritchie, 2007). In a purely PhD by independent study, the collaboration is mostly between doctoral students and their research supervisors. This usually takes the form of a mentor–mentee apprenticeship. In such cases, the initial collaborations may be deemed as asymmetrical with the doctoral student mentee assuming the role of a novice learning from their expert supervisor mentor (Ritchie, 2007). Collaborative research relationships, according to John-Steiner (2000), develop over time and are therefore dynamic. The once-novices in a research relationship can evolve to view themselves on equal footing with their supervisor mentors.

In Aleta's case, the relationship building was experienced early in her PhD v.2.0 journey when she was an online distance student. This occurred through her supervisor's consistent actions and direction to other members of her learning community who were equally committed to provide much-needed support as described in Chap. 4. Through consistent feedback and engagements with the learning advisor, the negative impacts of PhD v.1.0 and the self-perceived difficulties not only in academic writing but in the research process itself were alleviated. The result was an increase in Aleta's confidence and positive developments in her sense of self as a researcher.

5.2.1   Trustbuilding in a Collaborative Research Culture

Key to shaping effective collaborative research relationships is the development of trust. This is evident in Aleta's experiences during her PhD v.1.0 and PhD v.2.0. One of the significant contributions of this book is its examination of the relationships between research students and their support team. A better understanding of this can assist in the development of relationship building techniques that engender trust throughout the research journey and ultimately result in successfully written theses and well-established student-researcher identities. This knowledge can benefit students, academic institutions, supervisors, and support staff seeking to enhance research student success and identity development.

In terms of the student-supervisor relationship, Jacobsen et al. (2021) discuss the importance of trust as a meta-condition and that it should be established early in the relationship. Gasson and Bruce (2019) also recognize its importance and emphasize the development of collaborative research cultures, focused on trust and respect, to ensure student success during the research journey. Their collaborative research culture framework (Gasson & Bruce, 2021) covers three aspects of the research process, namely roots of collaboration (self as researcher, within research community, and beyond research community), fields of collaboration (informal network, formal research community, and sanctioned research community), and fruits of collaboration (inspiration, innovation, and inclusion). The roots of collaboration are established in trust and respect—dual concepts that also permeate the fields and fruits of collaboration. In terms of research collaboration, trust can be defined as "a confidence in revealing vulnerability to others" (Gasson & Bruce, 2019, p. 191). This vulnerability represents a risk and uncertainty, that overtime can be overcome through positive experiences of trusting others (Gasson & Bruce, 2019). As outlined by Douglas above, risk and uncertainty can be especially acute for research students during the conceptualization and writing phases of the research journey. In this case, the roots of collaboration were established through Douglas' collegial and collaborative approach. This meant that the necessary trust and respect were present so that Aleta felt confident to reveal vulnerabilities and therefore was able to receive further thesis improving feedback.

Conceptualization and writing are particularly sensitive aspects of a project where the student can feel vulnerable and at risk of ridicule, failure, and the unpleasant reality that the project is not quite right yet. Jacobsen et al. (2021) outline the significance of each of these in establishing good student-supervisor relationships. They identify "formative, iterative and timely feedback" and "collaborative community of support for academic writing" as significant enabling factors in this process (Jacobsen et al., 2021, p. 637). These must be built on relational trust and are vital for project conceptualization and the continual development of ideas (Jacobsen et al., 2021).

5.2.2 Self-Determination Theory and Research Collaborations

In the research collaboration, supervisors and other significant support staff need to be aware of the issues regarding conceptualization and writing and provide support in ways that motivate student success through developing trust and limiting vulnerabilities. Self-determination theory provides a suitable framework to determine different supervisory styles and assess more effective approaches to student support and success (Devos et al., 2015). As such, many studies have used the framework to better understand research students' motivational processes as part of doctoral education (De Clercq et al., 2021; Devos et al., 2015; Kumar & Kaur, 2019; Litalien & Guay, 2015; McCarthy, 2016). In reflecting on the experiences of Aleta, outlined above, we suggest that self-determination theory can be used to build relational trust and respect that benefits the student across all aspects of the research student journey, including individual competence, motivation, and confidence within research student relationships and collaborations.

Self-determination theory examines social, cultural, and biological factors in order to determine what contributes to, and what detracts from, human wellness and success (Ryan & Deci, 2017). To achieve this, the theory focuses on the basic psychological needs of competence, relatedness, and autonomy (Ryan & Deci, 2017). Autonomy is the ability for individuals to make their own decisions that align authentically with their interests and values (Ryan & Deci, 2017). Although much of what we do is governed by internal and external pressures (Ryan & Deci, 2017), when we have agency in the decision-making process, our decisions and motives are more aligned and we are more likely to feel better within ourselves about pursuing a particular course of action. Competence is a need to feel mastery and a required level of ability to operate effectively within a specific context (Ryan & Deci, 2017). We are motivated by our belief in our ability to undertake tasks and achieve related goals and outcomes. This also means motivation can be adversely affected by overly negative feedback or personal comparison or criticism focused on the individual which may create feelings of inadequacy and incompetence (Ryan & Deci, 2017). Relatedness refers to feelings of social connectiveness and the effects this has on motivation through an individual's feelings of belonging, being cared for, social significance to others, and level of contribution to the group (Ryan & Deci, 2017).

Following the tenets of self-determination theory, if research students are to thrive, they need social connection, capability building, and to feel in control of their own decision-making. Throughout Aleta's PhD v.2.0 experiences with her supervisors and a third-space academic such as a researcher development specialist and learning advisor, Douglas, elements of self-determination theory were evident in developing trust and limiting vulnerabilities. This was especially true regarding the feedback she received on her ideas and her writing. Social connection was provided through a network of support. This was not just her supervisors but a larger support group that included, administrative support, the Library Research Support Team, other research students within the Research and Writing League and the Postgraduate and Early Career Research group, and specialized writing support. This created a team of like-minded individuals that Aleta could connect with to feel she belonged in the research space. It was important that this space was one in which she not only felt supported to achieve her own research goals but that she also felt socially significant as an emerging researcher capable of contributing to the international research space and her home institution in the Philippines. This capability was built over time through feedback delivered in constructive ways that aligned with self-determination theory and sought to emphasize existing capability and build on this. Social connection and capability were achieved alongside autonomy, in that Aleta's relationships and research progression involved two-way discussion of multiple options and provided the skills for her to make decisions for herself based on the options provided.

Through the autoethnographic reflections of Aleta and Douglas it is apparent that trusting collaborative relationships are important elements for a successful student research journey. This chapter demonstrates the significance of this, especially in terms of the thesis writing aspects. Approaches that emphasize autonomy, competence, and relatedness, as outlined in self-determination theory, are conducive to building trust and enhancing wellbeing. This is important for a student's collaborative relationship with their research supervisors and, as Aleta's experience outlines, just as significant in interactions with other staff within university support services. As such, these types of approaches should be encouraged and actively fostered not just for supervisors but with all staff involved in a research student's journey. A lot of emphasis has been focused on the supervisor and to a lesser extent the institutional, role in postgraduate research study. Aleta's journey provides a lens from the student perspective and demonstrates the need for initiatives that provide research students with the knowledge and skills to develop, nurture, and assess respectful and trusting collaborative research networks. The ability to recognize positive and negative aspects within collaborative research cultures and respond accordingly can have a large impact on project conceptualization, writing, and ultimately researcher development and project success. If Aleta had been afforded these skills earlier, her PhD v.1.0 may have been a more productive experience, or at the very least a shorter one.

References

Andersen, N., Bremner, M., Derrington, K., Eacersall, D., Gunton, L., Howarth, D., Howlett, A., Jeffers, M., Pearse, T., Pickstone, L., Piper, S., Sahay, A., Sherwin, L., Stagg, A., Thangavelu, E., Thorpe, C., & Tweedale, R. (2021). *USQ library stories of 2020*. University of Southern Queensland. https://usq.pressbooks.pub/2020libraryreport/

De Clercq, M., Frenay, M., Azzi, A., Klein, O., & Galand, B. (2021). All you need is self-determination: Investigation of PhD students' motivation profiles and their impact on the doctoral completion process. *International Journal of Doctoral Studies, 16*, 189. https://doi.org/10.28945/4702

Devos, C., Van der Linden, N., Boudrenghien, G., Azzi, A., Frenay, M., Galand, B., & Klein, O. (2015). Doctoral supervision in the light of the three types of support promoted in self-determination theory. *International Journal of Doctoral Studies, 10*, 439. http://ijds.org/Volume10/IJDSv10p439-464Devos1858.pdf

Eacersall, D. (2018). Quest for student success: An exploration of the academic skill needs of Higher Degree by Research students at a regional university. University of Southern Queensland. https://research.usq.edu.au/item/q74y8

Gasson, S., & Bruce, C. (2021). Collaborative research culture framework v5. https://researchonline.jcu.edu.au/71050/

Gasson, S. C., & Bruce, C. (2019). Supporting higher degree research collaboration. *Studies in Graduate and Postdoctoral Education, 10*(3), 189–199. https://doi.org/10.1108/SGPE-04-2019-0040

Jacobsen, M., Friesen, S., & Becker, S. (2021). Online supervision in a professional doctorate in education: Cultivating relational trust within learning alliances. *Innovations in Education and Teaching International, 58*(6), 635–646. https://doi.org/10.1080/14703297.2021.1991425

John-Steiner, V. (2000). *Creative collaboration*. Oxford University Press.

Kumar, V., & Kaur, A. (2019). Supervisory practices for intrinsic motivation of doctoral students: A self-determination theory perspective. *International Journal of Doctoral Studies, 14*, 581–595. https://doi.org/10.28945/4415

Litalien, D., & Guay, F. (2015). Dropout intentions in PhD studies: A comprehensive model based on interpersonal relationships and motivational resources. *Contemporary Educational Psychology, 41*, 218–231. https://doi.org/10.1016/j.cedpsych.2015.03.004

McCarthy, G. (2016). Applying self-determination theory to improve completion rates in a part-time professional doctorate program. In *Emerging directions in doctoral education* (Vol. 6, pp. 207–223). Emerald Group Publishing Limited. https://doi.org/10.1108/S2055-364120160000006018

Ritchie, S. M. (2007). *Research collaboration: Relationships and praxis.* Brill. https://doi.org/10.1163/9789087903138

Ryan, R. M., & Deci, E. L. (2017). *Self-determination theory: Basic psychological needs in motivation, development, and wellness.* Guilford Publications. https://doi.org/10.7202/1041847ar

Tobin, K. (2007). Creating and sustaining productive research squads. In S. M. Ritchie (Ed.), *Research collaboration: Relationships and praxis* (pp. 43–58). Brill. https://doi.org/10.1163/9789087903138_005

Villanueva, J. A. R. (2017, October 9). When the going gets tough, the Underwoods get going! *Scratch paper: Aleta's evolving quests, confusions and equilibrium.* https://thisisgettingitchy.blogspot.com/2017/11/the-underwoods-get-going.html

Villanueva, J. A. R. (2018, September 24). 19th month: No turning back. *Aleta's Scratch Paper@Mahara.* https://eportfolio.usq.edu.au/user/aleta-villanueva/aleta-villanueva

Villanueva, J. A. R. (2020a, January 26). Zoom 332057715 in my mind. *Scratch paper: Aleta's evolving quests, confusions and equilibrium.* https://thisisgettingitchy.blogspot.com/2020/01/zoom-332057716-in-my-mind.html

Villanueva, J. A. R. (2020b, February 20). A neat kind of nitpicking. *Scratch paper: Aleta's evolving quests, confusions and equilibrium.* https://thisisgettingitchy.blogspot.com/2020/02/a-neat-kind-of-nitpicking.html

Villanueva, J. A. R. (2020c, May 13). It's like this 3. *Scratch paper: Aleta's evolving quests, confusions and equilibrium.* https://thisisgettingitchy.blogspot.com/2020b05/its-like-this-3.html

Villanueva, J. A. R. (2020d, November 27). *Research journey: Ingress to Egress.* [Paper presentation]. 26th Postgraduate and Early Career Research Symposium, University of Southern Queensland, Toowoomba, Australia.

Conclusion: The End is the Beginning

Abstract This chapter provides final discussions and conclusions for key issues identified in the book. The important themes, uncovered as part of the autoethnographic reflections throughout—the student research journey as an expression of the self; a reflective practice; a rite of passage; and as a collaborative act, are discussed with particular emphasis on the ways in which the research student journey can be better understood and improved. Improving the research experience increases student success across many aspects of the research journey including the development of research and employability skills, a significant and original contribution to the field of research, a more enjoyable and healthy experience, growth for the student's own identity and more productive and enduring relationships within, and with, the institution.

Keywords Doctoral Education · Research student · Student experience · Student success · Researcher identity · Higher degree by research, HDR · Postgraduate Research, PGR · Research culture · Learning alliance · Community of Inquiry, CoI · Research supervision · Self-determination theory, SDT

The collaborative autoethnographic account in this book outlines a doctoral research journey, through the reflections of the student herself (Aleta) and additional insights from an academic and researcher development specialist (Douglas), who shared in a part of that journey. Aleta's journey included multiple attempts to complete her PhD at two institutions—one in her home country of the Philippines and one in a regional area of Australia. It was at this regional university that Aleta successfully completed her PhD. Her journey to completion was a long but significant one and encompassed many relevant aspects of the student research journey, including project conceptualization, different supervisory approaches, proposal defense and Confirmation of Candidature, institutional support or lack thereof, research writing, identity development, research cultures and research collaborations. It is reflective of many of the significant issues in postgraduate research education, including timely completion, low completion rates, and student experience and wellbeing. Identity trajectory theory (McAlpine, 2012) and the Community of Inquiry (CoI) framework (Garrison et al., 1999) were used to better understand Aleta's experience in order to

  71
J. A. R. Villanueva and D. C. F. Eacersall, *Autoethnographic Reflections on a Research Journey*, SpringerBriefs in Education, https://doi.org/10.1007/978-981-99-4929-8

learn from and improve the student research journey. As a result of this type of reflection and findings, student success can be enhanced through timely degree completion, researcher identity development, increased positive collaborative research cultures and consideration of student wellbeing, as well as improved student confidence, agency, and capability.

As part of the research process, the following themes were identified: the research journey as an expression of the self; a reflective practice; a rite of passage; and as a collaborative act. The findings within these themes highlight significant points and raise important questions for the development and further refinement of postgraduate research training. This is specifically the case in the areas of 'research as an expression of the self' in terms of project conceptualization and refinement; 'research as a rite of passage' and its effect on researcher identity and wellbeing; and 'research as a collaborative act' especially in relation to more holistic collaborative research relationships broader than the supervisory team. Consideration and reflection in these areas can improve institutional approaches, supervisor quality and additional support mechanisms to benefit research student experience, wellbeing, and ultimately enhance the quality and quantity of research outputs and subsequent generations of researchers.

Research as an Expression of the Self – Project Conceptualization and Refinement

Choice of research topic is an important and challenging part of the research student journey (Hill & Mohammed, 2020; Russell, 1996). As demonstrated through Aleta's story, it can have important implications for research student experience, future career aspirations, and researcher identity. There is some confusion regarding the best approach when choosing a student research project. It has been suggested that selecting a topic that is aligned to the supervisor's area of research has positive effects for student satisfaction and retention but that freedom of project choice is also highly valued by research students (van Rooij et al., 2021). Employability after the degree has also been suggested as an important consideration, with projects aligning to career interests and aims being more desirable than those with little relevance to future career direction (Sharp et al., 2017). Researchers have also suggested several models and research topic generation tools to assist students with project selection (Pandit & Shah, 2017), and there are suggestions for supervisors to assist students with research topic development through defining titles, research questions, and conceptual frameworks (Wisker, 2012). There is very little discussion in the literature on the implications a sense of self and/or personal investment in the topic has on topic selection, project feasibility and identity.

In Chaps. 1 and 2, Aleta's and Douglas' reflections demonstrated that personal investment in the research topic can have both positive and negative effects on the student research journey. In terms of the positive, these types of topics can carry significant meaning for the researcher and their developing researcher identity. Often related to a student's past experiences and sense of self they can be strongly connected to where the student feels they came from and the direction they feel they are heading. This aligns with the ideas of identity-trajectory where a singular identity is developed through "changes in perceptions, emotions, knowledge, and abilities over time through experiencing life" (McAlpine & Amundsen, 2018, p. 27) and incorporates "students' pasts and imagined futures" (McAlpine, 2012, p. 38). In these cases, a student whose topic is closely entwined with their sense of self may be more motivated to undertake the research and to persist and successfully complete it, even if the journey is difficult. A student's personal investment in the topic can also result in more particular feelings of connection and a significant contribution not just to knowledge but to project participants and stakeholder groups. Each of these was reflected in the experiences of Aleta and formed part of this autoethnographic account. The downside, in terms of this type of connectedness to the project, is mainly related to the project's conceptualization and resulting feasibility. Although in our experience, proposed student research projects often have initial conceptual issues, student projects where the student is personally invested in the topic can be more predisposed to issues of scope and bias and the student less open to necessary refinements. Students can initially have research project ideas that are too large in scope. These often entail worthy and noble ideals but are too ambitious for the parameters of a single research degree. Feelings of loss and disappointment can emerge when students realize their project cannot achieve everything they had hoped it could. Personally invested topics can also be more prone to bias. This is because the personal meaning of these topics may be closely related to the researchers own personal experience. This can result in the project being shaped by preconceived anecdotal conclusions. This can also mean that students are less open to suggestions and refinement of their topic as it is closely tied to their personal experience and their sense of self. Refinement of the topic to meet institutional and disciplinary requirements can be difficult as changes to the topic feel like a denial of the self and elements of what the student hopes to achieve. These types of issues all represent conceptual concerns, the refinement of which can result in a longer and a more difficult journey for the student.

In comparing Aleta's experiences between PhD v.1.0 and PhD v.2.0 it is evident that she was personally invested in each of the associated topics. In terms of project conceptualization, what made PhD v.2.0 more successful was a more balanced approach in terms of personal investment and the requirements of the degree. This was due to a more refined topic shaped by her learnings over time as an academic in the Philippines and through guidance provided by her supervisors and others at her Australian institution of study. This was a case of learning and identity development intertwining over time to shape her project to align with her emerging sense of self as a student, academic, and researcher. The result was a feasible project that resulted in successful completion of her degree. We argue that balance is vital to enhance the positive aspects and limit the negatives when considering the connection between research and the self, and project conceptualization. The institution, research supervisors, and the student must all work together to ensure that expectations are clear and that provisions are in place so that students are aware of, and receive, the necessary supports to successfully refine their research topic and associated researcher identity.

Research as a Rite of Passage—How Challenging Should Research Be?

The student research journey has been likened to a rite of passage (Amran & Ibrahim, 2012; Kiley, 2009; Raineri, 2013). This analogy defines postgraduate research as an experience in which the student passes from one state to another—entering as novice and emerging transformed as a more capable researcher. Using Meyer and Land's (2006) notion of threshold concepts and Turner's (1967) work on liminality, Kiley (2009) suggests that students can get caught in a number of smaller rites of passage or thresholds and that these represent states of liminality. These states of liminality are spaces 'betwixt and between' (Turner, 1967), where the student may experience difficulty moving from one stage to another. Difficulties in a research degree can result in negative impacts on student success and wellbeing (Beasy et al., 2021; Brownlow et al., 2022; Sverdlik et al., 2018) but also signify periods of growth and learning once the threshold has been passed. Considering this and the way in which Aleta arrived at her viable research topic, raises another very important question—was the length and difficulty—the 'rite of passage'—she experienced in arriving at her topic, and eventually completing her research degree, a necessary, or even desirable, part of the research process?

On reflection throughout the chapters of this book, the difficulties Aleta faced throughout her 'rite of passage' shaped her final successful topic and many of the positive aspects of the researcher identity she currently assumes. One of the most admirable of these being her desire to act on concrete plans as an academic in her institution in the areas of teaching and extension work to include programs and activities (Figs. A.1 and A.2) to help fellow teacher educators and research students avoid some of the pitfalls and negative aspects she experienced in her PhD v.1.0. The struggles she experienced, wrestling with the literature, and refining and further refining her ideas into a viable project enabled her to develop important researcher attributes such as critical thinking, resilience, and persistence. Aleta's story, throughout the chapters of this book, demonstrates how these experiences molded her into the person and researcher she is today.

On successfully attaining their degrees, graduates of research programs tend to look back on even the most traumatic of journeys and, with a sigh of relief, proclaim that it was worth it. Although we realize that the difficulties of the journey make the student researcher who they are and that researcher identity is developed through a particular set of circumstances—the good and the bad, we argue that research is difficult at the best of times and that the 'rite of passage' should be a positive experience involving constructive learning experiences and adequate support, guiding

Fig. A.1 A montage of Aleta's activities during and post-PhD v.2.0. *Note.* Adapted from Villanueva (2020), *"Research journey: Ingress to egress"*

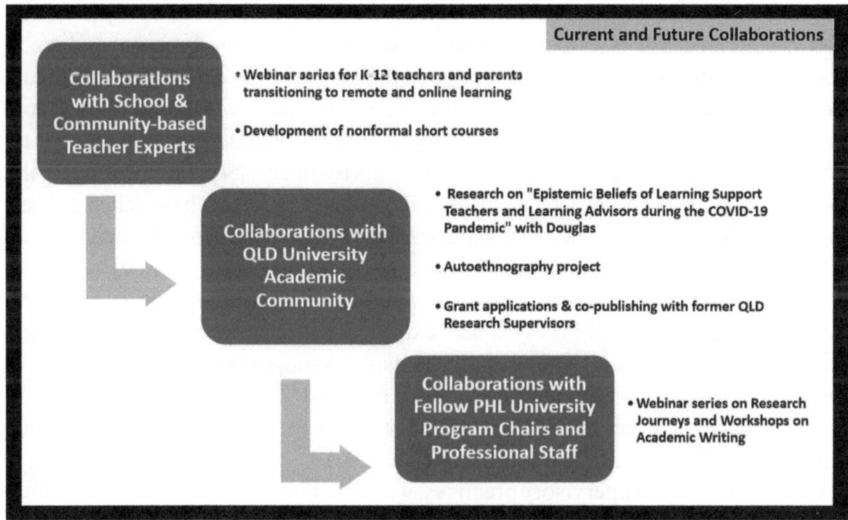

Fig. A.2 A screenshot of action plans from Aleta's 26th PGECR presentation. *Note.* Adapted from Villanueva (2020), *"Research journey: Ingress to egress"*

the 'right to safe passage' from student to competent researcher. As Aleta's experience shows, a difficult journey and resultant researcher identity are not so productive if the trauma has negatively impacted the student's timely completion, wellbeing and mental health. We can learn from the experiences of others to ensure pitfalls are avoided and better paths are taken, resulting in a more productive and enjoyable journey. Adequate support, facilitating a 'right to safe passage' is vital in this process to ensure student success and that students can pass through difficult aspects of the journey unscathed. This support involves 'research as a collaborative act' and consideration of research relationships and learning alliances.

Research as a Collaborative Act—Relationships and Alliances

Effective collaborative research cultures are important in providing appropriate support and guidance to research students. This is relevant for finding a viable topic and the entire student journey and experience from admission to final completion. In discussing this area, research supervision, holistic approaches, relational methods, and the role of the institution must be considered.

The supervisory relationship plays a significant role in the postgraduate research student journey. Dependant on its quality, it can have both positive and negative effects on the student experience (González-Ocampo & Castelló, 2019; Sidhu et al., 2013; Skakni, 2018; Wadesango & Machingambi, 2011; Woolderink et al., 2015). Through Aleta's experiences it is evident that when supervision is good the experience is improved but when supervision is not so good the journey can be more difficult. In the case of good supervision, experiences can be anything from wonderful to mediocre and in terms of supervision that is lacking they can be disastrous and damaging for all involved. Although there have been improvements to supervisory training (e.g., in the Australian context see Kiley, 2011), historically many supervisors have relied on their experiences of being supervised, or supervising with an 'experienced' supervisor to inform their supervisory practices (Bastalich, 2017; Hammond et al., 2010). Again, the effectiveness of this situation relies heavily on the quality of the supervisor's own experience and the abilities of the 'experienced' supervisor. We suggest that effective training for supervisors and mechanisms to support and encourage them to constantly aspire to improve their practice are required. Supervisors should take full advantage of all the training opportunities afforded them including both institutional training and individualized learning (Fulgence, 2019).

As part of effective supervisory practices, we argue that supervisor training emphasizes approaches grounded in educational pedagogy (e.g., see Bastalich, 2017). Since the 2000s, Australian institutions have seen an increase in this approach (Kiley, 2011), leading to more transparent supervisory practices (Hammond et al., 2010) and less reliance on personal experience informing individual supervisor approaches (McEachern, 2004). As Aleta's experience emphasized, supervisory practice can benefit from a focus on student research training as a student-centered learning experience and process of identity development rather than a supervisory dominant and/or research project objectives driven approach. This research suggested a CoI style-approach taking into account teaching presence, cognitive presence, and social presence in the training of research students. This approach has seldom been used in doctoral education research (e.g., see Lambrev & Cruz, 2021). We argue that supervisor training with this type of focus will assist in reducing the number of negative experiences and will also increase the quality of student experiences that may have otherwise been mediocre. Supervisor training that makes supervisors more cognizant of student experiences, such as Aleta's—difficulties with project conceptualization, a lack of clarity regarding administrative processes and research, and the importance of learning theories such as the CoI framework can assist in improving the student experience.

Even with effective supervisor training initiatives, overreliance on supervisors in the research student learning journey is problematic. One of the major contributions of our autoethnographic account is the importance of developing research cultures that encourage a range of effective relationships in the research student journey and how these can be established and fostered for the benefit of the student. We argue that effective supports from not just supervisors but also significant others including colleagues, family, the institution, and research support specialists play a significant role in developing positive student experiences and identity development. This should take a learning alliance approach (Halse & Bansel, 2012), where the main actors, student, institution, and supervisors, work together to ensure a successful journey. Holistic, learning alliance-type approaches can add additional layers of support to increase the probability of positive student experience. Building on this concept for joint responsibility between student, supervisors, and the institution, we argue that the university should be responsible for establishing and maintaining learning alliances, and that the obligations of the other main parties need to be clearly outlined and defined. Reflecting on Aleta's experiences, we feel this is necessary in order for the learning alliance to become a practical operational reality that benefits research students. Our research also suggests that in certain circumstances, colleagues, family, and friends represent significant others that should also be considered in the learning alliance approach.

Other important aspects, emphasized by our study and related to the learning alliance and developing a positive research culture, include university support services, networking opportunities, and student involvement in researcher groups. Aleta's lived experience demonstrated that consultations with research support specialists and involvement in activities such as writing groups, researcher societies, conferences and symposiums build community and through enhancing cognitive, social and teaching presence, support student success. Community and research cultures have been discussed as a way for research students to successfully pass through liminal stagnation points (Kiley, 2009) and can create a sense of belonging and relatedness shown to improve student satisfaction and retention (van Rooij et al., 2021). As evident in Aleta's experience they also broaden the student's support networks and represent interactive research cultures of sharing and support. These types of research cultures ensure that there are sufficient supports in place so that if any one aspect fails there are still elements to assist the student in their endeavors. When all the elements are in play, research cultures and interactive networks are developed that ensure an optimal research study experience.

In Aleta's case, research writing groups were especially useful networks for peer support and learning. These can be an effective means of support for research students, providing collaborative learning communities that encourage a "sense of belonging through self-reflection and the sharing of experiences in a safe space, which builds perceived self-efficacy and self-awareness" (Hradsky, et al., 2022, p. 16). They enable students to develop important skills with other research students, thus establishing writing and skill development as a social practice, that can occur outside of the supervisory team (Chakraborty et al., 2021). Therefore, we recommend that institutions emphasize the provision of learning communities, such as writing groups, mentoring programs, peer study groups, researcher societies, research support specialists, and student symposiums and conferences to ensure the provision of a holistic study experience for research students.

The autoethnographic account of lived experience in this book suggested that, within these relationships and research cultures, certain styles of interacting foster valuable elements of respect and trust. These were Douglas' 5-step approach and the integration of self-determination theory into approaches to research student training. Douglas' suggested method included active listening, genuine empathy, providing options rather than solutions, assisting students with action plans, and being mindful of students' wellbeing. This is a student-centered approach designed to engender trust, through respecting students and their needs. It aligns well with the tenets of self-determination theory. Self-determination theory focuses on the basic psychological needs of competence, social relatedness, and autonomy. Student autonomy is particularly relevant here as approaches that emphasize student agency demonstrate confidence in students' abilities to make decisions for themselves and therefore reflect respect and trust in the relationship. Approaches that emphasize student agency have positive effects on student satisfaction (Shin et al., 2018; van Rooij et al., 2021) and retention (van Rooij et al., 2021). We agree with others such as van Rooij et al. (2021) and Overall et al. (2011) that there is a need to balance freedom and autonomy within structures that still provide students with adequate support and direction, but recommend that this should be extended beyond just the supervisory relationship to include all student interactions across the institution.

Although research has focused on supervisory relationships and self-determination theory (De Clercq et al., 2021; Devos et al., 2015) we suggest that the overarching principles of these types of approaches—student agency, competency and social involvement, aligning with meeting student needs, in student-centered, respectful, and trusting ways can also be applied more broadly across the institution. In this way, it could be used as a philosophy to inform policy and approaches to research student training and development for research management, supervisors, and more general support staff, such as, research training specialists, librarians, and administration professionals. We argue that institutions should foster cultures that encourage approaches such as these in order to facilitate research success and positive research journeys. If this strategy is taken, then effective research relationships can be established, maintained, and utilized for the collective benefit of all involved.

This autoethnographic work provides an account of the student research journey. Through a collaborative process we have reflected on the student experience and made a significant contribution to research student training and development. The findings of this research will benefit research students, supervisors, research support staff, higher education institutions and policy. Specifically, our reflections contribute to the growing literature on student experience from a student perspective; approaches to research project conceptualization; an understanding of student researcher identity development; supervisor training; and collaborative student research cultures. Our reflections will assist the major stakeholders to have a better understanding of the higher degree educational journey. Current and prospective students will have a better understanding of the research process, how to approach it and what to do if things are going wrong; research supervisors and support staff will approach research student support in ways that focus on student learning needs; and institutions will develop research cultures that foster positive research relationships. In this way, our research contributes significantly to increased student success in the form of successful completion, research outputs, and employability, as well as a more enjoyable research journey leading to happy, healthy and confident research students with a corresponding researcher identity. It is our hope that this research will not just offer advice and recommendations but that it will also encourage further discussion and research in these areas, including additional student accounts to add to the growing literature on research student experience.

References

Amran, N. N., & Ibrahim, R. (2012). Academic rites of passage: Reflection on a PhD journey. *Procedia-Social and Behavioral Sciences, 59*, 528–534. https://doi.org/10.1016/j.sbspro.2012.09.310

Bastalich, W. (2017). Content and context in knowledge production: A critical review of doctoral supervision literature. *Studies in Higher Education, 42*(7), 1145–1157. https://doi.org/10.1080/03075079.2015.1079702

Beasy, K., Emery, S., & Crawford, J. (2021). Drowning in the shallows: An Australian study of the PhD experience of wellbeing. *Teaching in Higher Education, 26*(4), 602–618. https://doi.org/10.1080/13562517.2019.1669014

Boylorn, R. M., & Orbe, M. P. (Eds.). (2014). *Critical autoethnography: Intersecting cultural identities in everyday life* (1st ed.). Routledge. https://doi.org/10.4324/9781315431253

Brownlow, C., Eacersall, D., Nelson, C. W., Parsons-Smith, R. L., & Terry, P. C. (2022). Risks to mental health of higher degree by research (HDR) students during a global pandemic. *PloS ONE, 17*(12), e0279698. https://doi.org/10.1371/journal.pone.0279698

Chakraborty, D., Soyoof, A., Moharami, M., Utami, A. D., Zeng, S., Cong-Lem, N., Hradsky, D., Maestre, J. L., Foomani, E. M., & Pretorius, L. (2021). Feedback as a space for academic social practice in doctoral writing groups. *Educational and Developmental Psychologist, 38*(2), 238–248. https://doi.org/10.1080/20590776.2021.1972764

De Clercq, M., Frenay, M., Azzi, A., Klein, O., & Galand, B. (2021). All you need is self-determination: Investigation of PhD students' motivation profiles and their impact on the doctoral completion process. *International Journal of Doctoral Studies, 16*, 189. https://doi.org/10.28945/4702

Devos, C., Van der Linden, N., Boudrenghien, G., Azzi, A., Frenay, M., Galand, B., & Klein, O. (2015). Doctoral supervision in the light of the three types of support promoted in self-determination theory. *International Journal of Doctoral Studies, 10*, 439. https://doi.org/10.28945/2308

Fulgence, K. (2019). A theoretical perspective on how doctoral supervisors develop supervision skills. *International Journal of Doctoral Studies, 14*, 721. https://doi.org/10.28945/4446

Garrison, D. R., Anderson, T., & Archer, W. (1999). Critical inquiry in a text-based environment: Computer conferencing in higher education. *The Internet and Higher Education, 2*(2), 87–105. https://doi.org/10.1016/S1096-7516(00)000 16-6

González-Ocampo, G., & Castelló, M. (2019). How do doctoral students experience supervision? *Studies in Continuing Education, 41*(3), 293–307. https://doi.org/ 10.1080/0158037x.2018.1520208

Halse, C., & Bansel, P. (2012). The learning alliance: Ethics in doctoral supervision. *Oxford Review of Education, 38*(4), 377–392. https://doi.org/10.1080/03054985. 2012.706219

Hammond, J., Ryland, K., Tennant, M., & Boud, D. (2010). *Building research supervision and training across Australian universities: Final report*. Australian Learning and Teaching Council. https://dro.deakin.edu.au/articles/report/Bui lding_research_supervision_and_training_across_Australian_universities_final_ report/20910757/1/files/37185220.pdf

Hill, C., & Mohammed, M. (2020). The challenges of conducting qualitative research: Student perspectives from the United Arab Emirates. *Journal for Researching Education Practice and Theory, 3*(1), 84–116.

Hradsky, D., Soyoof, A., Zeng, S., Foomani, E. M., Cong-Lem, N., Maestre, J-L, & Pretorius, L. (2022). Pastoral care in doctoral education: A collaborative autoethnography of belonging and academic identity. *International Journal of Doctoral Studies, 17*, 1–23. https://doi.org/10.28945/4900

Kiley, M. (2009). Identifying threshold concepts and proposing strategies to support doctoral candidates. *Innovations in Education and Teaching International, 46*(3), 293–304. https://doi.org/10.1080/14703290903069001

Kiley, M. (2011). Developments in research supervisor training: Causes and responses. *Studies in Higher Education, 36*(5), 585–599. https://doi.org/10.1080/ 03075079.2011.594595

Lambrev, V. S., & Cruz, B. C. (2021). Becoming scholarly practitioners: Creating community in online professional doctoral education. *Distance Education, 42*(4), 567–581. https://doi.org/10.1080/01587919.2021.1986374

McAlpine, L. (2012). Identity-trajectories: Doctoral journeys from past to present to future. *The Australian Universities' Review, 54*(1), 38–46.

McAlpine, L., & Amundsen, C. (2018). *Identity-trajectories of early career researchers*. Palgrave Macmillan. https://doi.org/10.1057/978-1-349-95287-8

McEachern, D. (2004). A balance between the pursuit of excellences and real world needs of students. In M. Kiley & G. Mullins (Eds.), *Quality in postgraduate research: Re-imagining research education* (pp. 45–52). Centre for the Enhancement of Learning.

Meyer, J., & Land, R. (Eds.). (2006). *Overcoming barriers to student understanding: Threshold concepts and troublesome knowledge.* Routledge. https://doi.org/10.4324/9780203966273-9

Overall, N. C., Deane, K. L., & Peterson, E. R. (2011). Promoting doctoral students' research self-efficacy: Combining academic guidance with autonomy support. *Higher Education Research & Development, 30*(6), 791–805. https://doi.org/10.1080/07294360.2010.535508

Pandit, H. B., & Shah, D. B. (2017). A model of decision support system for research topic selection and plagiarism prevention. *The International Journal of Engineering and Science, 6*(1), 40–42. https://doi.org/10.9790/1813-0601024042

Raineri, N. (2013). The PhD program: Between conformity and reflexivity. *Journal of Organizational Ethnography, 2*(1), 37–56. https://doi.org/10.1108/joe-04-2012-0021

Russell, A. (1996, April 18–19). Postgraduate research: Student and supervisor views. Quality in postgraduate research: Is it happening?, Adelaide Australia.

Sharp, J. A., Peters, J., & Howard, K. (2017). *The management of a student research project.* Routledge.

Shin, J. C., Kim, S. J., Kim, E., & Lim, H. (2018). Doctoral students' satisfaction in a research-focused Korean university: Socio-environmental and motivational factors. *Asia Pacific Education Review, 19*(2), 159–168. https://doi.org/10.1007/s12564-018-9528-7

Sidhu, G. K., Kaur, S., Fook, C. Y., & Yunus, F. W. (2013). Postgraduate supervision: Exploring Malaysian students' experiences. *Procedia-Social and Behavioral Sciences, 90*, 133–141. https://doi.org/10.1016/j.sbspro.2013.07.074

Skakni, I. (2018). Doctoral studies as an initiatory trial: Expected and taken-for-granted practices that impede PhD students' progress. *Teaching in Higher Education, 23*(8), 927–944. https://doi.org/10.1080/13562517.2018.1449742

Sverdlik, A., Hall, N. C., McAlpine, L., & Hubbard, K. (2018). The PhD experience: A review of the factors influencing doctoral students' completion, achievement, and well-being. *International Journal of Doctoral Studies, 13*, 361–388. https://doi.org/10.28945/4113

Turner, V. (1967). Betwixt and between: The liminal period in rites de passage. In V. Turner (Ed.), *The forest of symbols: Aspects of Ndembu ritual* (pp. 93–111). Cornell University Press.

van Rooij, E., Fokkens-Bruinsma, M., & Jansen, E. (2021). Factors that influence PhD candidates' success: The importance of PhD project characteristics. *Studies in Continuing Education, 43*(1), 48–67. https://doi.org/10.1080/0158037X.2019.1652158

Villanueva, J. A. R. (2020, November 27). *Research journey: Ingress to Egress.* [Paper presentation]. 26th postgraduate and early career research symposium, University of Southern Queensland, Toowoomba, Australia.

Wadesango, N., & Machingambi, S. (2011). Post graduate students' experiences with research supervisors. *Journal of Sociology and Social Anthropology, 2*(1), 31–37. https://doi.org/10.1080/09766634.2011.11885545

Wisker, G. (2012). *The good supervisor: Supervising postgraduate and undergraduate research for doctoral theses and dissertations.* Bloomsbury Publishing.

Woolderink, M., Putnik, K., van der Boom, H., & Klabbers, G. (2015). The voice of PhD candidates and PhD supervisors. A qualitative exploratory study amongst PhD candidates and supervisors to evaluate the relational aspects of PhD supervision in the Netherlands. *International Journal of Doctoral Studies, 10*, 217. https://doi.org/10.28945/2276